W0215253

Developing User Assistance for Mobile Applications

Joe Welinske

Developing User Assistance for Mobile Applications

Copyright © WritersUA

All rights reserved. No part of this work may be reproduced or transmitted in any form or by any means, electronic or mechanical, including photocopying, recording, or by an information storage or retrieval system, without the prior written permission of the copyright owner and the publisher.

ISBN: 978-1-257-50372-8

Trademarked names may appear in this book. Rather than use a trademark symbol with every occurrence of a trademarked name, we use the names only in an editorial fashion and to the benefit of the trademark owner, with no intention of infringement of the trademark.

President and Publisher: Joe Welinske
Cover Designer: Chris Barbee
Editors: Sue Heim and Karen Ziegler

The information in this book is distributed on an "as is" basis, without warranty. Although every precaution has been taken in the preparation of this work, neither the author nor the publisher shall have any liability to any person or entity with respect to any loss or damage caused or alleged to be caused directly or indirectly by the information contained in this work.

110609

To Shan, George, and Em —
The trio who make me more proud and content
every day we're together

Contents

Acknowledgements vii

1 ***User Assistance in a Mobile World*** ***1***
What this Book is NOT About 2
There is a Role for UA in Mobile 3
The Mobile UA Skill Set 8
Take-away and Preview 11

2 ***Getting Started*** ***13***
Get a Smartphone 13
Using Simulators/Emulators 15
Tablets 15
Emerging Devices 16
The Device Acquisition Conundrum 16
Take-away and Preview 17

3 ***Designing for Mobile User Assistance*** ***19***
UA Content for First-time Users 20
Guided Help 22
UA in a Dedicated Help Section 23
Videos and Demos 28
UA in Multiple Forms 29
Take-away and Preview 31

4 ***Creating Helpful Words and Images*** ***33***
The Language of Gestures 33
Using Language in UI Elements 37
Writing Procedures 41
Messaging 46
Video Tutorials 47
Image Formats 49
Take-away and Preview 50

5 ***Browser-based Help*** ***51***
Browser Compatibility 51
Designing a Help Template 52
Context-Sensitive Help 57
Help Authoring Tools 58
Testing Tools 66
How to Deliver Your Help 68

6 iPhone and iPod Touch (iOS) *71*
Hardware/Software 71
Knowledge 72
Interface Builder 72
Learning About Objective-C 78
Learning About WebKit / Safari 78
Working with a Project in the Simulator 79
Importing a Provisioned App 80
Screen Captures from an iOS Device 81
Screen Captures from OS X 81
The Safari Debug Console on iOS 82
Translation 82
Miscellaneous Resources 83

7 Android *85*
Hardware/Software 85
Installing the Android SDK 86
Android Virtual Devices 89
User Interface Text 93
Screen Captures from an Android Device 94
Android-based Tablets 95

8 Windows Phone *97*
Hardware/Software 97
Installing the WP7 SDK 97
User Interface Text 104
Screen Captures 105

9 The iPad and Tablets *107*
Designing UA for Tablets 108
Working with the iPad 115
Working with Android-based Tablets 117

10 Integrating with Other Types of User Assistance *119*
Integrating with a Desktop Application 125
Desktop App Stores 127

About the Author

Joe has been involved with software documentation development since 1984. He founded and produces the WritersUA Conference for Software User Assistance which has drawn thousands of attendees over its twenty years. Together with Scott Boggan and David Farkas, Joe authored the popular and pioneering book *Developing Online Help for Windows 95*.

He has taught at the University of Washington in the Department of Technical Communication, the University of California at Santa Cruz, and Bellevue Community College. Joe served as President of the Puget Sound Chapter of the Society for Technical Communication and as Membership Director for the Puget Sound Chapter of the Usability Professionals Association. He was awarded the Myron L. White award as an International Leader in Technical Communication by the University of Washington. He is an Associate Fellow of the Society for Technical Communication.

Joe received a B.S. in Industrial Engineering from the University of Illinois in 1981. He received a Master of Education specializing in Adult Instructional Management from Loyola University in 1987. In his spare time, he likes to travel, kayak, and write.

Acknowledgements

Discussions with my colleague, Professor David Farkas, provided many ideas for this book. He also took the time to review the manuscript and offer many useful suggestions. Sue Heim was very generous with her time in editing the content. Karen Ziegler did a great job copyediting.

I received many useful suggestions from those who attended my series of webinars on this topic. Several of them reviewed a preview version of this book and supplied me with great feedback.

1 User Assistance in a Mobile World

The ubiquity of cell phones means that almost all of us have experienced mobile voice calling and texting: instant communication with anyone, anytime. We are used to getting what we want extremely fast and in just the way we like. Most consumers have brought those same expectations with them as they move to smartphones (Fig. 1.1) and mobile applications (apps.) The apps of today are all about speedy access to discrete actions and specific information. This is a very different environment from the fixed workstation, large-screen desktop environment of traditional enterprise applications.

Fig. 1.1

There is no question that smartphones have sparked a huge, new software segment – the mobile app. The Apple iTunes App Store (Fig. 1.2) hosts hundreds of thousands of apps that have been downloaded billions of time and generated billions of dollars in revenue. Google's Android operating system is now in the hands of more consumers than any other smartphone and has a growing inventory of apps. Windows Phone 7 (hereafter referred to as "WP7") is off to as strong a start as the iPhone had four years ago. Other names like Blackberry, HP/Palm, and Nokia are making moves to get a piece of the app action as well. There are not many computer/software organizations that don't have a mobile strategy for their products and services.

Fig. 1.2 iTunes App Store

According to the independent Pew Research Center, "The mobile device will be the primary connection tool to the internet for most people in the world in 2020." The next few years is going to see a very rapid conversion in the IT industry in the way software is designed, implemented, and consumed. This creates an important pair of questions for user assistance (UA) professionals: What is our role going to be in mobile and how can we prepare to take that on?

This book is based on practical experience working with a variety of mobile apps and their associated development frameworks. It is a distillation of challenges and solutions encountered with respect to design, technology, and implementation. The work has included iPhone, iPad, and Android apps. Additional experience has been with WP7, Nokia/Symbian, and RIM/Blackberry. Hopefully this book will prove to be a useful guide for the user assistance community.

The links and image from this book are available on the WritersUA web site. Content updates will be posted there as well.

- ***Developing UA for Mobile Apps*** **site:** http://www.writersua.com/mobile/

What this Book is NOT About

Many organizations are employing smartphones as an eReader for reference information such as those shown in Fig. 1.3. For example, a field technician working on a piping system might have all of the latest service manuals available on an iPhone. Or a sales rep might have a list of equipment specifications in an app on a Droid. An HR manager might carry around all of the company policy and procedure manuals on a tablet. There are many great reasons to deliver documentation through mobile devices. That is a different category of technical communication and this book doesn't try to address it.

Fig. 1.3 Reference materials on mobile devices

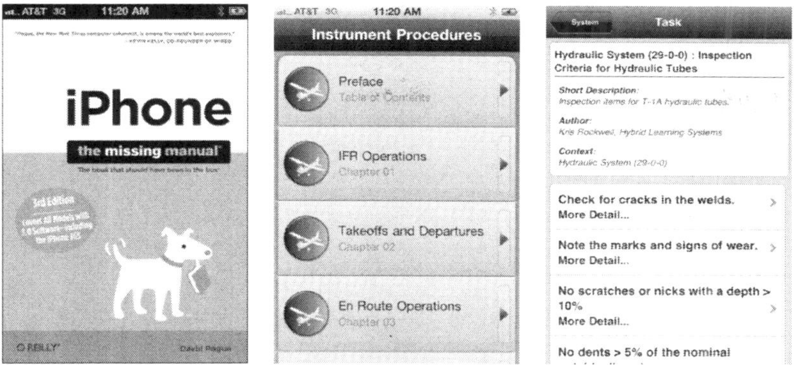

There is a Role for UA in Mobile

There is no question that there is a role for user assistance in the mobile world. Our skills and experience are definitely applicable. But the nature of many of our deliverables is likely to be very different from what we have done in the past.

The single most important lesson of this book might be that bringing over Help designs from desktop applications is a really bad idea. The most useful and interesting user assistance approaches try to match the environment of the apps they support.

This book showcases a number of examples of mobile user assistance. Gordon Meyer of Apple has also put together a nice collection of "Help" for iPhone apps. One of the few unifying characteristics of the many examples is that they don't use designs brought over from Windows and desktop applications.

- Gallery of iPhone Help: http://www.g2meyer.com/gallery/main.php?g2_itemId=5026

The iPhone, Android, and WP7 are successful because the designers recognized that the mobile user environment is very different from the desktop. Mobile app developers tend to be very sensitive to the differences between mobile and desktop software. If you try to bring your desktop Help designs into a team meeting, you may find a lot of people rolling their eyes.

As user assistance professionals, we need to break away from the traditional online Help designs and consider what it means to be mobile. The best mobile UA is going to be where the UA content is customized, as closely as possible, to the user experience of individual apps as closely as possible. This may not always be possible, but it should definitely be the ideal.

Complexity and minimal screen real estate don't easily mix

The current crop of smartphones is limited by the amount of space on the screen. Some devices have crept up to a larger viewing area. Others have worked on improving the resolution of the screen. As tablets emerge, we have a form factor that is somewhere between a smartphone and the desktop.

Ultimately we are dealing with a small viewing/work area. This affects our ability to embed user assistance in the app. It is often a struggle to wrangle UA space in desktop applications. In mobile, it is even tougher. Our UA solutions have to really shine to get a place in the apps.

Fig. 1.4 illustrates the problem. The amount of screen space on a smartphone is dwarfed by the amount available on a typical desktop monitor. This is slightly offset on some smartphones with the use of high-resolution displays. Even so, it is still a significant challenge to present information to the user on smaller devices.

Fig. 1.4 Comparison of screen sizes (values are vertical heights)

Multi-touch and multi-key controls are not easily discoverable

Many mobile apps are using multi-touch gestures to trigger certain features. For example, pressing and holding in a certain part of the screen will popup a control box. A double-tap might have a different function than a single-tap.

Fig. 1.5 shows three multi-touch examples. In Quickoffice, a touch and hold on a dividing line between two rows will activate a control for increasing/decreasing row height. In PhotoPad, once an image is displayed in the editor you can touch and hold to crop the image or pinch to shrink it. In AccuTerra, you need to tap a placeholder icon to reveal the name associated with that marker.

Fig. 1.5 Multi-touch examples

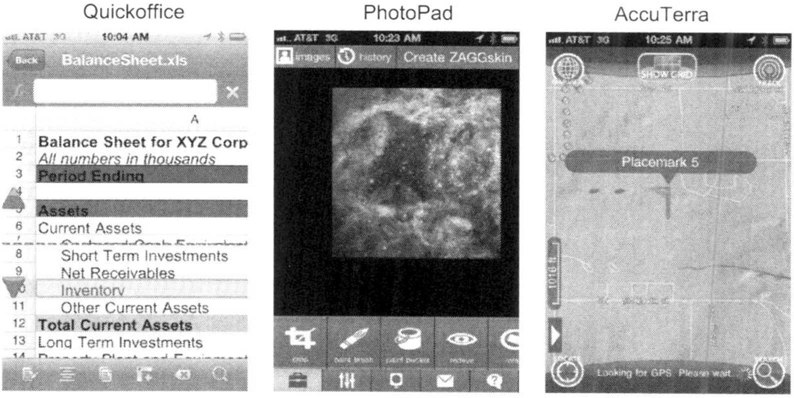

How do those concepts get communicated to first-time users? It is a difficult problem to solve. Part of it is technical and part of it is design. On the technical side, there are limitations on how information is presented to the user in certain contexts. On the design side, we need to come up with a good solution for explaining multi-touch gestures. We are also again confronted with minimal screen real estate.

Whether or not hidden features are in the best interest of the app is a broader question for the whole development team to discuss.

Conceptual, contextual information is still important

One of the unsung areas of software documentation has always been conceptual information. You can argue that a more intuitive UI minimizes the need to explain about clicks and taps. But how does a user learn what the software can do to help her in solving a problem at work or play?

The 99-cent price of many apps makes it a no-brainer to just download and try them out. At higher prices, users are likely to want more information if they can't try before they buy. If an app has many features, it makes sense to have user assistance that addresses this. This might take the form of a tour, a video, or Help section that may or may not be embedded in the app itself.

For corporate apps, there is a high level of urgency in this area. It is of value to your organization that an employee knows how to effectively use a mobile app in their work. Fig. 1.6 shows the Chevy Dealer Mobile Workbench. This is an on-the-go version of a desktop application that salespeople use at the dealerships. A web-based video describing how the mobile app works can be integrated with the tools they are already familiar with. The five or ten minutes a user spends with an instructional video will pay off many times over through more effective use of the mobile app.

Fig. 1.6 Chevy Dealer Mobile Workbench web video

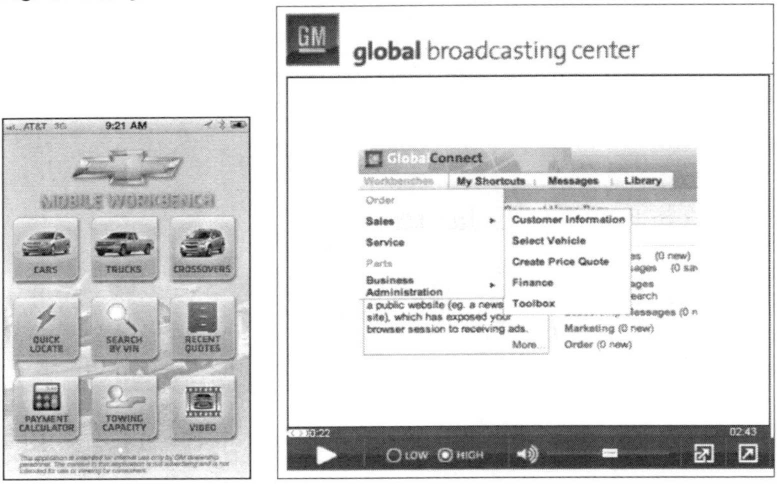

- Chevy Dealer Workbench web site:
  http://gbc.feedroom.com/?fr_chl...rf=sitemap

More apps are appearing that are robust and "corporate"

The most popular mobile apps tend to be basic in terms of what they can do. The ones in the iTunes Top Ten lists tend to be for mainstream consumers and consist mostly of games and widgets. If you dig deeper, you start to find paid apps that offer more functionality.

What you don't see in the app store is the growing number of apps that are "sidecars" to full-featured enterprise applications. You will find many of these examples in this book. The corporate categories include banking, automotive, healthcare, and engineering.

Within those categories are functional areas like human resources, sales, and customer service. Many if not most of these apps, are available on iTunes, yet are password-protected, and require a prior relationship with the organization. One of the biggest UA challenges is to provide a seamless, consistent user experience between mobile and desktop applications.

Fig. 1.7 shows apps that provide mobile customer service. They support a broader relationship with the customers. For example, the Safeco Insurance and MyHumana apps are for customers who already have purchased insurance with the company. Ingram Micro is a very large European wholesaler of technology products.

Fig. 1.7 Apps for customer support

Safeco Insurance MyHumana Mobile Ingram Micro Mobile

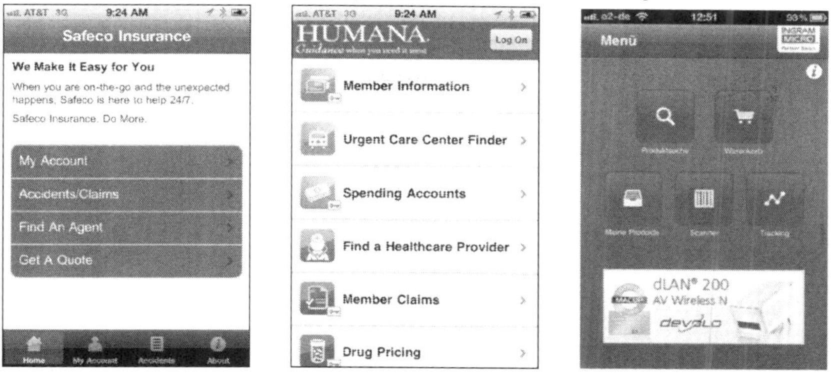

Fig. 1.8 shows examples of apps that provide functionality tied to other products and services. The apps were developed to help boost customer satisfaction with those products and services. HP ePrint lets you use your mobile device to send a print job to a remotely located, web-connected printer. TotalConnect lets Honeywell customers remotely control an alarm system. System administrators can manage servers remotely with IBM Mobile Systems Remote.

Fig. 1.8 Apps tied to other products and services

HP ePrint Service TotalConnect IBM Mobile Sys. Remote

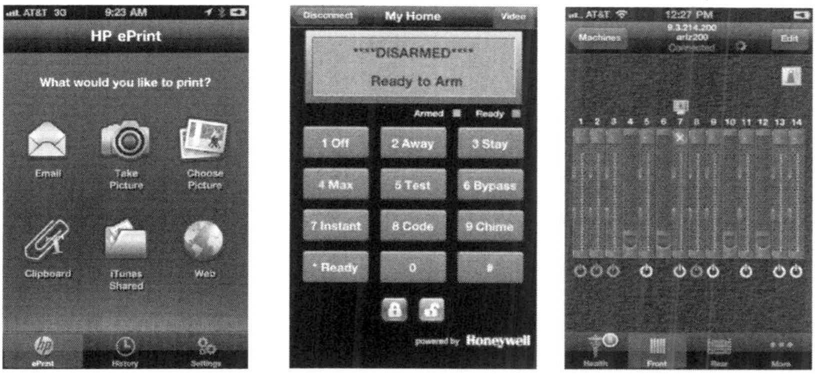

Fig. 1.9 shows examples of corporate apps that offer a variety of specialized services. Raytheon uses an app to regularly post job listings. Cisco provides a tool for testing Internet speed. The Intel Retail Edge Program app helps salespeople keep up on the latest product offerings.

Fig. 1.9 Corporate apps

RaytheonJobs | Cisco Global Internet | Intel Retail Edge Program

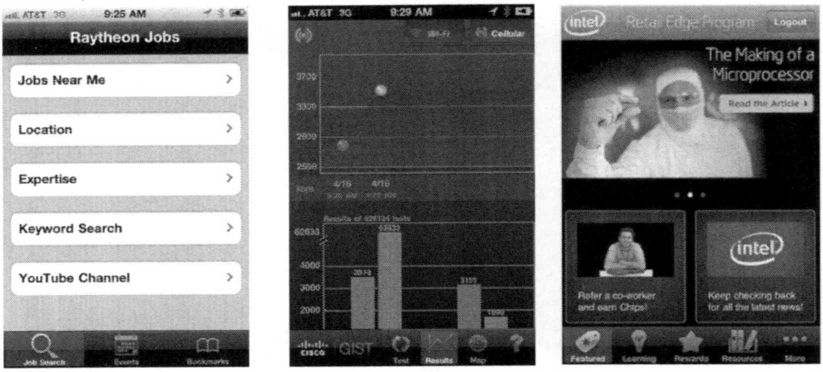

The Mobile UA Skill Set

If you have been involved with user assistance for traditional software applications, you are in a good position to move into support for mobile UA. If you are new to the discipline, you will find it useful to learn the fundamentals of technical communication. While mobile apps represent a new way of thinking about software development, most of the skills involved with desktop application development are still very relevant.

Designing the UA

Many of the general categories of user assistance for desktop applications apply to mobile. These include tutorials or guided assistance for first-time users, embedded helpful information in the user interface, and the creation of a section of more detailed Help info. An app might use one or more of these approaches. The difference from traditional UA lies in how those items are executed or accessed. This is discussed in more detail in Chapter 3: *Designing for User Assistance.*

An important skill for mobile UA is usability testing. Even the smallest elements of an app can have a disproportionate effect on whether a customer enjoys the app or not. The very fact that mobile devices are mobile makes it easy to present apps to people for testing. The simulators available for the various mobile platforms provide a great way to make quick user interface iterations – largely without the assistance of a programmer. There is a huge body of information available about what usability testing is and how to do it well.

- Usability Professionals Association: http://www.upassoc.org/

The *most* important design skill might just be thinking outside the box. Apps represent a significant break from decades of software design. The best apps creatively envision new ways for people to work on the go. Our user assistance needs to match that creativity by moving away from the legacy designs of fixed workstation computing. One of the least useful entities is the venerable "Help system" with its navigation hierarchy and repository of topic pages.

Creating content

There are countless quotes by famous people along the lines of Mies van der Rohe's "less is more." This concept definitely applies to mobile UA. Effective UA for apps is more about crafting words and phrases and less about generating volumes of content. Large-scale documentation probably doesn't have a place in the mobile world. That being said, our foundation skills of writing, editing, task analysis, and SME interviewing are still extremely important. This idea is discussed in more detail in Chapter 4 : *Creating Helpful Words and Images.*

In mobile, writing is about spending more time coming up with precisely the right words. During the editing process, the emphasis must be on strictly limiting the volume of text while maintaining quality and usefulness. Knowing the customer and the task at hand are still critical to developing the right UA approach. Procedures, reference information, wizards, embedded Help, and user interface text are still key elements. They just have a very different form factor in mobile.

Knowledge of information design and content management is going to help your overall mobile UA effort. However, many of the processes used to support traditional software development may be too unwieldy for mobile purposes. For example, mobile UA emphasizes embedded, brief content. It would be difficult to manage this with most of today's content management systems. In the coming months and years, keep an eye out for evolving best practices.

The use of well-crafted images and video is definitely part of today's mobile UA. This is an area on which to spend more time.

Indexing and search techniques are of less use in mobile. If a user needs to search for Help content, then the user assistance material is probably far too extensive.

Building digital deliverables

For much of the past two decades, an important aspect of user assistance has been converting our designs and content into a digital format for consumption by our users. This includes creating HTML Help, support pages on a web site, or embedded text in the user interface. While the look and feel of these deliverables has changed with mobile apps, ultimately we are still working with software.

There are a couple of key process differences from desktop application development. One is the rapid iteration/evolution of operating systems. The other is the high-level of control imposed by platform gatekeepers on how apps are compiled. What this boils down to is a constantly changing environment for how mobile apps are designed and built.

Experience with HTML, Cascading Style Sheets (CSS), and JavaScript continue to be important. A focus on HTML 5 is critical to working with the mobile platforms. The iPhone/iPad eco-system is already highly dependent on HTML 5. Using CSS helps to minimize the size of our code that is stored in an app and delivered over the air. Mobile is moving faster than the desktop in this area. Adobe's Flash has been shut out of the Apple eco-system. It is not clear if it will have a place in mobile apps.

Understanding how apps are built can really make the difference in how effective you are in your UA efforts. The technical limitations and opportunities of mobile apps are very different from desktop computing. Programmers are really good at sniffing out whether we have any clue as to the challenges involved in building software. It is to your benefit to learn as much as you can. Fortunately, the development tools for mobile are very accessible and relatively easy to use. Several chapters in this book get into the specifics of turning your content into digital deliverables.

It is always a very good idea to learn a programming language. Once you've learned one it is easier to get at least a working understanding of others. Understanding how programming works makes it easier to communicate with developers. It also gives us the chance to dig into code on our own when we need to find something. Objective-C and C are the languages of choice for iPhone/iPad. Java is the bulwark of Android. Windows Phone 7 is based on C# with graphical apps relying on Silverlight.

Other areas of interest

One of the fun things about user assistance is that there are so many peripheral disciplines that align with our core competencies. Some of these areas map to mobile UA more than others.

Localization/Translation: Mobile apps have a variety of language strategies but they might not easily fit in with existing desktop production schemes. Text expansion due to different languages is an important consideration.

Instructional Design and eLearning: The use of tutorials and videos definitely fits into the mobile arena. The difference is scale. How do you embed training of content into a mobile environment? How do you adjust length and detail for an on-the-go experience?

Agile Development: The creation of mobile apps is fast-paced and highly iterative – almost by definition. If anything, a team needs to be even more tightly integrated when putting together a mobile app.

Structured Authoring / DITA: Organizing our valuable content is always a good thing. Separating content from presentation also has a lot of merit. The question is whether a process like structured authoring or a framework like DITA is useful in a setting where large-scale documentation is ill-advised. A related issue is if and how traditional content management systems can be adapted to support mobile development.

Help Authoring Tools: The very different nature of UA for mobile means that we need to look to very different types of tools for creating that UA. The Help designs for desktop applications are generally not suitable for mobile UA. Tools that only support those kinds of designs are not likely to be very useful.

Social Media: There are many ways that user assistance can employ the collaboration and community building of Twitter, YouTube, Facebook, and similar entities. Mobile apps are generally always "on-line" so it makes sense to integrate social media wherever appropriate.

With the exception of Localization / Translation, the areas described here are beyond the scope of this book. Cast a wide net to capture all the relevant developments in these fields related to mobile.

Take-away and Preview

User assistance has an important role in the development of mobile apps. However, it may be difficult to identify opportunities. It is important to look beyond mainstream apps and search out apps tailored to specific business contexts. Keep a look out for emerging mobile development in your own organization.

As you begin to work with mobile apps, try to disengage from legacy design and implementation techniques from the desktop world. Look at this as a completely new medium and tailor your UA accordingly. There are many unique challenges including screen real estate and multi-touch gestures.

Your past experience with UA will be extremely valuable. Fundamentals of communication still apply to mobile. Usability testing may be the most important skill to acquire and hone.

The next chapter discusses the current landscape of smartphones and other mobile devices. It offers recommendations for acquiring and upgrading devices for your own development needs.

2 Getting Started

Everyone needs to start somewhere.

Get a Smartphone

If you're serious about working with mobile apps, you need to get one or several mobile devices. Developing Help for a mobile app without having a smartphone would be like creating help for a desktop app if you could only view the app on a TV. You can probably get it done but it is not likely to result in great user assistance.

The smartphone line-up

If you are buying a smartphone mainly for your own personal use then the world is your oyster. There are dozens of choices out there for you. However, if you're buying one with an eye on learning about mobile UA, you need to give it a more focused consideration. You'll need to balance the high cost of the devices and associated service contracts against the value it can provide for your professional use. Hopefully the organizations that employ us will start buying smartphones devices for us to work with just as they provide us with desktop workstations. Fig. 2.1 shows a snapshot of market share for smartphones in the United States and the world.

Apple is definitely the juggernaut when it comes to the combination of the number of devices sold and the number of apps available. Now that Apple has both the iPhone and the iPad, the overarching operating system is referred to as iOS. Because the big money in apps is happening in iOS, that is where most developers are putting their first efforts. Unless your organization is specifically ignoring iOS, I would say it is the best place to start learning about mobile UA. There are really only two devices, the iPhone and iPad, and iOS supports both of them. In addition, Apple aggressively pushes their customers forward in updating on a regular basis. On the device front, there are few differences between the iPhone 3GS and 4. There even fewer differences between iPad and iPad 2. Overall, it is pretty easy to keep up with mobile developments in the Apple world.

Android just passed Apple in terms of the overall installed base of users for smartphones. However, that number is fragmented amongst dozens of devices and a half-dozen versions of the operating system. For developers, the tools and the marketplace are not as attractive as iOS. Android is the least likely place to look for apps that connect to traditional enterprise applications – at least right now. In addition, the tools for Android development are a lot trickier to work with than with than iOS. However, if you want to explore mobile apps in a relatively unrestricted but fast-moving ecosystem this is the place to be. There are also loads of unlocked, used Android phones available for sale.

Fig. 2.1a U.S. smartphone market share (Nielsen, Mar. 2011)

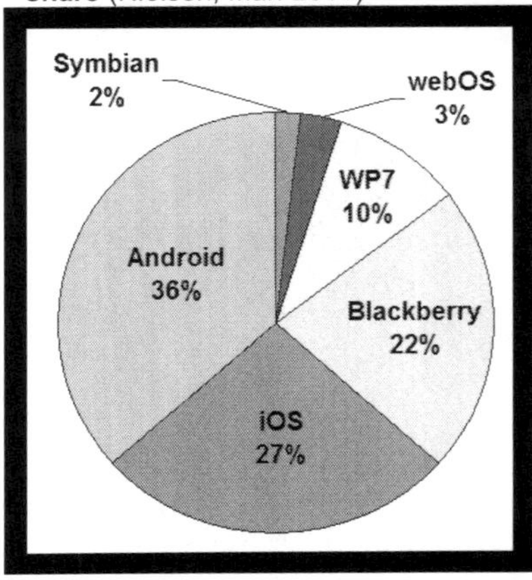

Fig. 2.1b World smartphone market share (Gartner, May 2011)

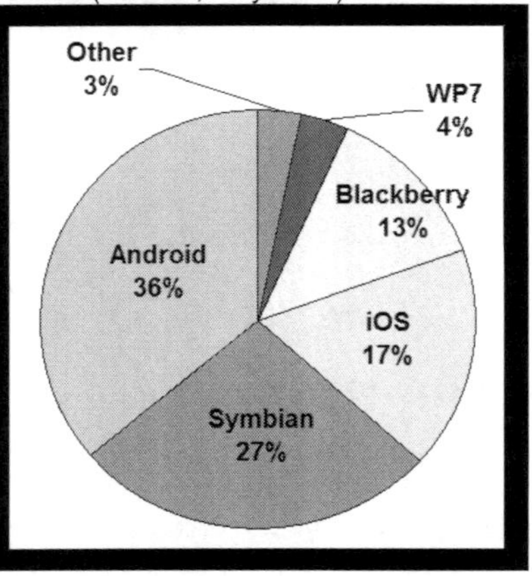

WP7 has not been flying off the store shelves. However, the user interface has received favorable reviews. It definitely presents an innovative point of view about what it means to have a smartphone. The partnership with Nokia should provide the momentum needed to move WP7 into third place in market share. If your company currently develops Windows applications, you may want to start your efforts with WP7. The WP7 developer tools from Microsoft are easy to use and free.

Most people who use Blackberry phones get them from their employer. If that is the case for you, then an upgrade to the latest models will keep you in the loop regarding mobile capabilities. However, the RIM app development strategy is moving slowly. Getting a Blackberry isn't going to help you learn much about mobile UA in the near future.

Nokia does not have a large presence with smartphones in the United States. Its early smartphone models have been somewhat uninspiring for consumers and developers. Part of that has to do with the slow evolution of the Symbian OS. The new partnership with Microsoft is likely to bolster the popularity of WP7 at the expense of Symbian. You might want to wait until the WP7/Nokia models come out before spending time in this area.

Using Simulators/Emulators

Most of the smartphone platforms provide simulators (see Fig. 2.2) so developers can test project changes quickly, without loading apps onto the associated devices. Simulators are a boon to user assistance professionals. They are fun to work with and allow you to experiment with designs without the help of programmers. Simulators are discussed extensively in this book. However, there are a few important limitations.

- There really isn't a substitute for working with the actual devices. You can't get a feel for ease of use, performance, and suitability to task through a simulator. It is also hard to understand why a person likes an iPhone over a Droid over an Evo until you play with them.

- Simulators are most useful if you have access to the project code for an app. A simulator can't display an app without the associated code. There are many scenarios where it might not be possible for you to get the code for the project you are working on. However, you can display browser-based Help in a simulator without project code.

- To use a simulator you need to install most, if not all, of the tools associated with a particular platform. You won't find any stand-alone simulators to use. You will need to learn the basics of the development tools in order to work with the simulators.

Fig. 2.2 iOS development with the simulator

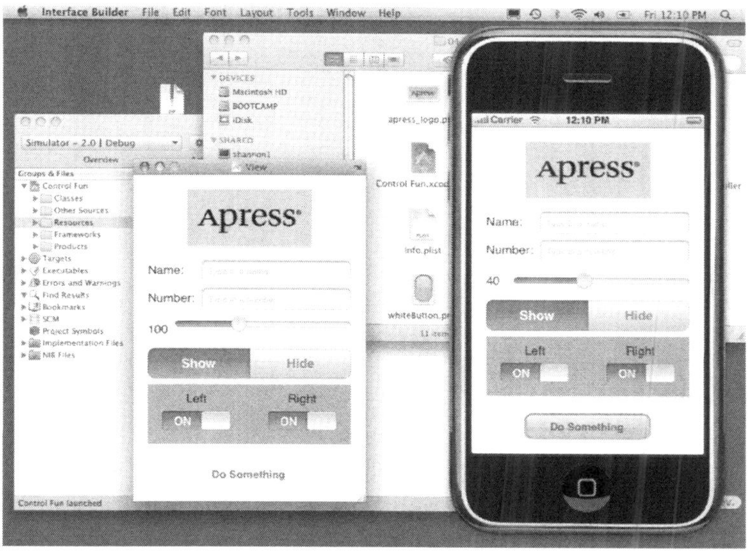

Tablets

The popularity of the iPad has been amazing. While tablet computers have been available for many years, it was Apple that finally captured the hearts of consumers. From the first release in the summer of 2010, the iPad was enormously popular and became a product behemoth in just over a year. For now, Apple owns this market. Although Motorola, Samsung, RIM, and many others are becoming more competitive, it will be a while before these devices come anywhere near approaching the success of the iPad. For more information, see Chapter 9: *The iPad and Tablets*, page 107.

Emerging Devices

The definition of "mobile" continues to evolve. Apps are appearing in new and surprising places. Ford and Toyota have created platforms for apps to be used in vehicles as shown in Fig. 2.3. We can expect to see more and more ways for mobile apps to be available to consumers.

Fig. 2.3

Ford Sync

Toyota Entune in Prius IV

The Device Acquisition Conundrum

Keeping up with mobile devices and applications is easier said than done. It is difficult to stay up-to-date with the ever-growing list of devices and associated operating systems. Just maintaining knowledge of iOS, Android, and WP7 is a struggle, not to mention the other platforms.

There are distinct differences on the surface of these environments and under the hood. WP7 has a completely different form factor from iOS, while Android is different from both of those. A person who buys an iPhone over a Droid is doing it for reasons beyond the cost of the device and the service contract. You can't effectively develop user assistance for a mobile app without understanding the nuances of the user interface and the expectations of the customer.

One of the challenges in keeping up with the device explosion is the cost of the devices. It isn't practical to have access to all possible devices. It might be difficult to justify having just one, let alone three or four of them. The average cost for a new smartphone is in the neighborhood of $500-600. In the United States, this cost is often subsidized by the telecommunication companies in exchange for taking on a two-year. service contract. Those contracts can easily cost $2,000-$3,000. Add to that the obnoxious practice whereby the networks hold back on software updates in order to boost the sales of new devices and extended contracts.

Most of us only need one contract – for our primary phone. It isn't practical to have multiple contracts. Most of us also cannot afford the retail, non-subsidized price for new phones. What is a UA professional to do?

One solution is to buy used, "unlocked" phones that are out of contract. The fast growth of the smartphone market means there is a burgeoning market for used, unlocked phones. You can find such devices on eBay for half the cost of what they cost new. If this is a supplementary device, you may be able to get along using the wi-fi capability only. Another option is to buy a pre-paid SIM card, which can usually be purchased for as little as $25. Pay-as-you-go internet access can work just fine for UA testing. Unlocking a phone can be a complicated and involved process. You are likely best off buying a phone that is already unlocked.

Beyond cost, there is the issue of updates. Apple has a pretty straightforward policy of pushing everyone forward at the same time on devices and software. The app development process follows Apple's release schedule very closely. The rigid control Apple has over their platform also means that developers don't have to deal with more than a couple variants in technology at any one time.

So far, version control hasn't been a problem with WP7, mainly because Microsoft hasn't been too swift with its updates. The first update came nearly six months after the first release.

Android is another story. From 2008 to early 2011, there have been six major updates with "sweet" names – from Cupcake to Honeycomb. The original Google phone was the G1 and it came out in 2008. It shipped with the first public release of Android, which was labeled 1.5 and called Cupcake. There was another update for 1.6 (Donut). However, the carrier T-Mobile, stopped shipping updates for this phone after 1.6. Even though this is an old phone, it is still capable of running later versions of Android.

In order to keep up-to-date at a reasonable cost, it may be necessary to "root" the phone and find open-source builds. This is an involved process but it gives you a lot of flexibility and maximizes the life of your investment in a device.

Take-away and Preview

If you are serious about mobile UA, you need to get yourself one or more mobile devices. You need to understand how mobile apps differ from the desktop. You also need an appreciation for the nuances of different platforms.

The cost of devices and connectivity contracts can be expensive. You'll need to do some careful research to find the solution that best fits your situation and budget. This might include purchasing, used, unlocked devices.

The next chapter reviews the UA designs of apps that are currently available. This should provide you with some practical examples of what works and doesn't work in the mobile space.

3 Designing for Mobile User Assistance

Designing user assistance content through mobile devices has two main challenges. One is coming up with a scheme for delivering assistance that satisfies the needs of the audience in a mobile environment. The second challenge is developing a system for generating the content that meets the specifications of the various devices you choose to support and the capabilities of your development team.

Consuming content on a mobile device is different from desktop PCs and TVs. You have limited screen size, varying form factors for interaction, and different expectations regarding the time and method for accessing the content. If the mobile app is linked to an enterprise-level software system, you also have the challenge of providing a seamless transition between desktop UA and the small device.

A key challenge is our ability to provide support for what has become an explosion of choice in devices and OS versions. There is a certain amount of dissonance here. On the one hand, people choose their mobile devices because they like the way one device works over another. An iPhone user is likely picking that device over a Droid or Blackberry for many reasons beyond price. Therefore, it makes sense to customize content for a device.

On the other hand, the practical implications of providing customization for so many devices are daunting. Finding the "sweet spot" for your customers and your development team becomes an important part of the design process. Cross-platform development needs to be part of the initial design discussions.

A good way to get a sense of which designs work and which don't is by looking at apps that have already been released. The following sections show examples in a number of user assistance categories. What you'll see is that the look and feel of the UA is as varied as the apps themselves. All of the designs have merit. Some achieve a better overall experience than others do. Most of these apps are available for free or 99 cents.

UA Content for First-time Users

Most mobile apps are easy to use. Some have more features than others. There might be nuances of an app that make it easy to work with over time once you know what to do. The first time a user works with an app might determine whether they continue with an app. At the 99-cent price level, apps could get discarded if they are not immediately intuitive.

The apps in this section have built in user assistance that appears the first time a user launches them. That information then falls away to the background.

ToonPAINT, shown in Fig. 3.1 ToonPAINT is an app that creates a cartoonish version of any photo. The first time you enter the app a graphical Help overlay appears. It shows the main gestures/tasks associated with the app. The graphical images (a. and b.) are very well done and show the needed interactions. The image you are working with shows through the Help, which keeps your task in context. After tapping the image, the Help goes away completely. A question mark icon displays an Info/Settings page. There is a reset control (c.) that lets you activate the Help info again.

Fig. 3.1 ToonPAINT

a. b. c.

Weightbot, shown in Fig. 3.2, lets you record your weight on a daily basis. You can look at graphs to see your progress over a period of time. The first time you enter the app it presents a welcome screen with a brief description. A graphical tutorial takes you through six panels of information. Breadcrumbs at the bottom indicate your progress. A Next button moves you forward in the tutorial. You can also flick forward and back. When the main app screen appears so does a simple popup listing the first step you need to take.

Fig. 3.2 Weightbot

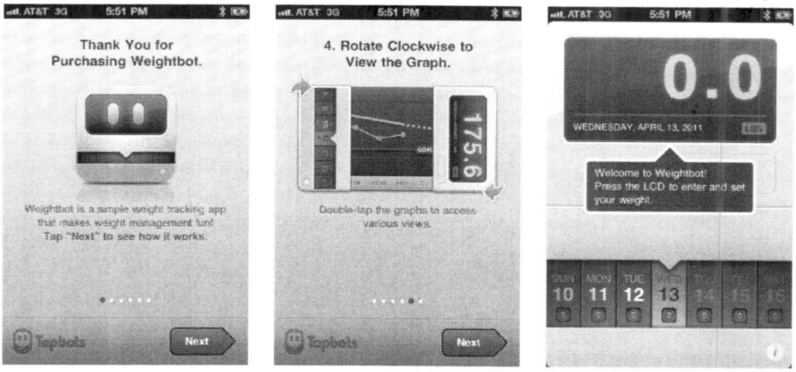

WebMD, shown in Fig 14, provides a wealth of medical information. On first use, a message appears asking if you want to take a tour of the app. This takes you through screen shots of the various sections of the app. It uses callouts to highlight important controls and gestures. The tour is always available to users. However, the welcome message appears only once.

Fig. 3.3 WebMD

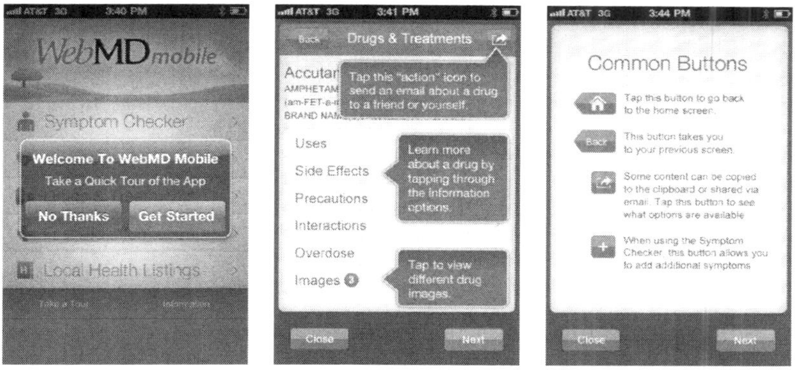

Fig. 3.4 shows three apps. **SoundHound** (a.) helps identify songs in a variety of ways. On first use, it presents popup balloons on the three main controls. When you tap any of the three, the whole Help display disappears. There is also a tiny "x" in the lower right corner of the lower balloon. This is another visual clue to dismiss the Help.

EpicWin (b.) is a daily task manager in the form of a game. Help tips appear on the main screen upon first use of the app. You win points for trying out the tips. This fits into the scheme of the app, which is that you win points for keeping up with your daily tasks. As you complete the tips, they disappear from the main page.

eBay (c.) offers a mobile version of its auction site. After doing your first search for a product, a popup appears showing you how to save the search. There is a reset button in Settings for displaying the Help again.

Fig. 3.4

a. SoundHound b. EpicWin c. eBay

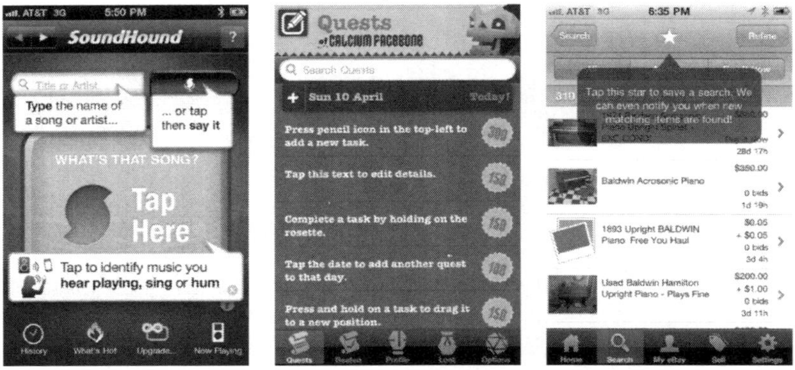

Guided Help

The closer that Help can be to the user interaction the more likely it is to be used. Guided Help is a term that applies to user assistance that is tightly connected to the user interface. It leads the user through a task without taking the user away from the task itself. Guided Help metaphorically holds the hand of the user in accomplishing tasks.

AutoCAD offers a mobile version of their computer-aided design software, shown in Fig. 3.5. When you select certain functions, guided Help text appears at the top of the screen. As you perform the steps, the Help phrases change. It doesn't appear that you can disable this feature. It might get tiring seeing the Help after repeatedly using the app. However, it doesn't slow down your ability to use the app.

Fig. 3.5 AutoCAD guided Help

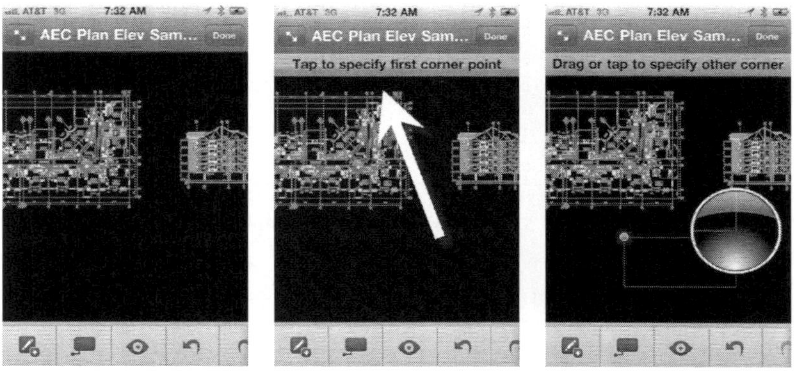

Google Search is shown in Fig. 3.6. If you click on the question mark in the top left corner of the home page (a.) the app goes into Help mode. A darkened overlay appears (b.) with question mark icons over all the clickable UI elements. Each of those icons brings up its own short Help phrase if you click on it (c.). The Close button in the top left corner removes the Help overlay. This technique addresses the situation where a screen might have a variety of possible user interactions.

Fig. 3.6 Google Search

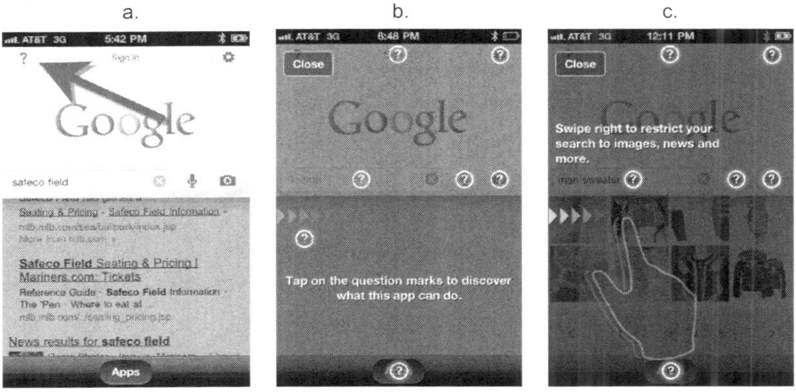

UA in a Dedicated Help Section

In most traditional desktop software applications, the Help information is collected in a single repository. This might be a compiled binary file or one or more web pages. The information collection usually consists of topic pages and navigation components to access those topics.

This form of UA is also found in mobile apps. Typically, some form of Help icon ⓘ is used in the main user interface. This links to one or more pages with the Help content. The Help information might be embedded in the native code of the app. It might also be an external set of web pages.

In either case, the use of this kind of Help system is much less effective than the options described in previous sections. It requires the user to leave the current position in the app and go on a hunt for the needed information. However, this option is often attractive to developers because it requires a reduced level of programming effort and support.

The **Starbucks Mobile Card** is shown in Fig. 3.7. This app shows how much money is available for purchase in your card account. It can also be used to make a purchase by scanning the app screen in the store. There is a Help item on the Settings page that leads to a three-level nested hierarchy of navigation links and topics.

Fig. 3.7 Starbucks Mobile Card

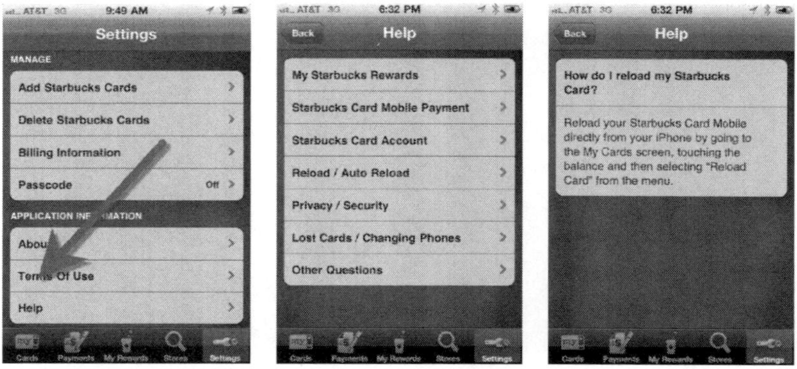

The topics might be improved by formatting the steps to be easier to read. Using the example in the right-hand panel:

> **To Reload Your Card:**
>
> On the **My Cards** screen, tap the balance.
>
> Tap **Reload Card**
>
> (etc.)

The pop-up Help used by **eBay** was described in the previous section. Fig. 3.8 shows the Help that is provided for sellers. A welcome page for sellers (a.) links to a "Getting Started Tutorial." It isn't really a tutorial, however. There are links (b.) to four very basic Help topics, one of which is shown (c.) in the figure. The navigation page is attractive and clear. The topic pages would probably be more effective if the action steps were presented in a procedural style. The prose paragraphs are lengthy and difficult to scan for key information.

There is also a link to videos. The link (b.) is described in the *Videos and Demos* section, page 19.

Fig. 3.8 eBay

a. b. c.

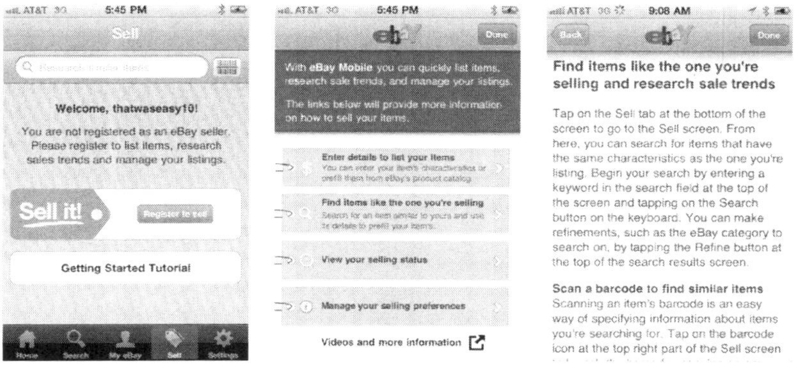

eTrade provides an app for its stock trading service, shown in Fig. 3.9. A Help button (b.) is included in the scrolling menu bar at the top. Because it is at the end of a list of twelve icons, it is not easily noticed when you first start using the app. The Help is a very long FAQ (c.) with no navigation links. It is difficult to find specific answers without reading through the whole page.

Fig. 3.9 eTrade

a. b. c.

Timewerks is shown in Fig. 3.10. This app provides a quick time tracking and invoicing tool for consultants/contractors. The "More" menu (a.) has a link to a Quick Start topic. This topic offers a quick overview of the major functions of the app. That topic uses a standard HTML hotspot to (b.) link to a step-by-step tutorial. The tutorial (c.) is short and to the point. It would be better if the information were presented to users when they first use the app.

Fig. 3.10 Timewerks

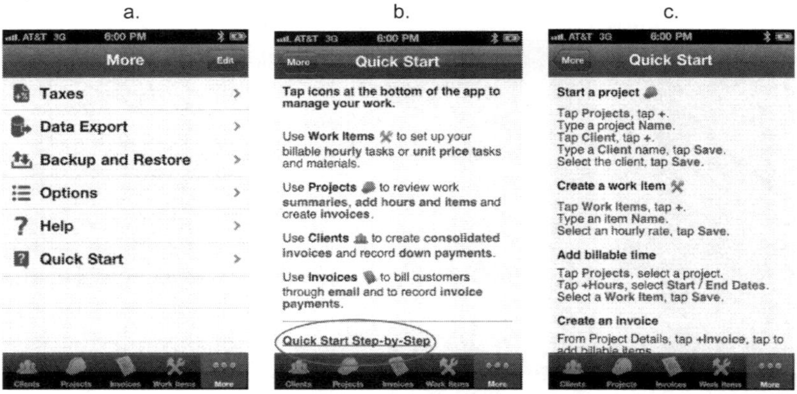

Calvetica, shown in Fig. 3.11, is a calendar app. The "starburst" icon in the top right (a.) links to a "Help & Settings" page. The icon does not really hint as to what it does. On the Help & Settings page (b.), the "How do I…" item branches to a long, single-page FAQ. The navigation links (c.) make it easy to move through the page. Font color helps to separate the Q's from the A's. The numbered steps are easy to follow.

Fig. 3.11 Calvetica

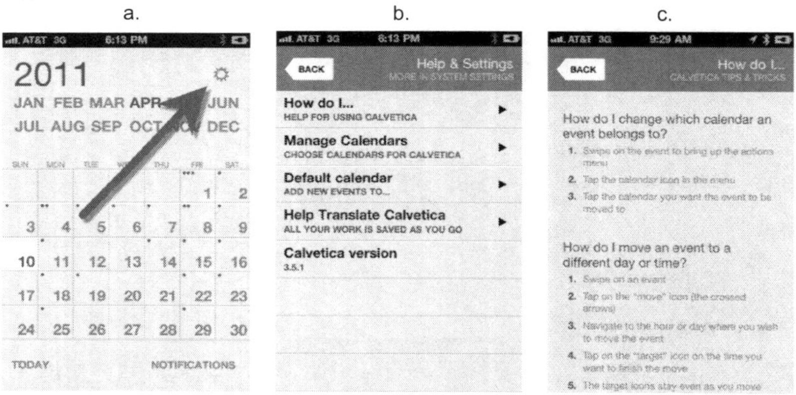

PhotoPad, shown in Fig. 3.12, is for manipulating images. A Help item (a.) is visible on the Tab bar at the bottom. The Help item links to a seven-panel series of topics. This includes a gesture graphic (b.), description of functions (c.), and FAQ. You can flick through the pages or use the browse arrows.

Fig. 3.12 PhotoPad

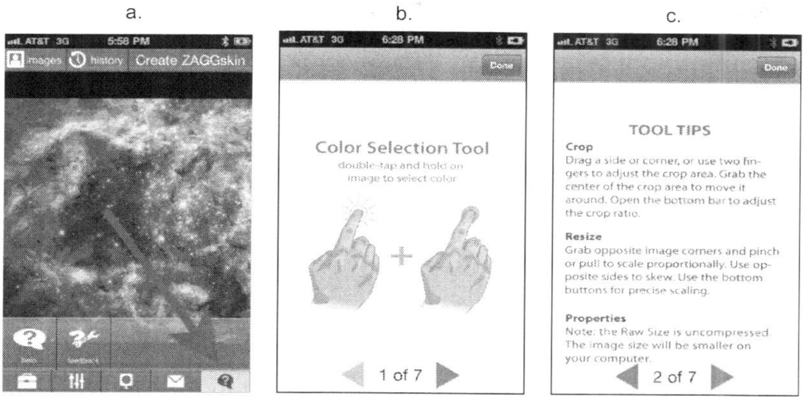

The **Amazon** app, shown in Fig. 3.13, provides the same purchasing services as the web site. Clicking "More" (a.) in the Tab bar displays a number of items. One of them is a Help link that leads to a three-level nested hierarchy of navigation links (b.) and topics. As with the Starbucks app, the topics (c.) might be improved by formatting the steps to be easier to read.

Fig. 3.13 Amazon

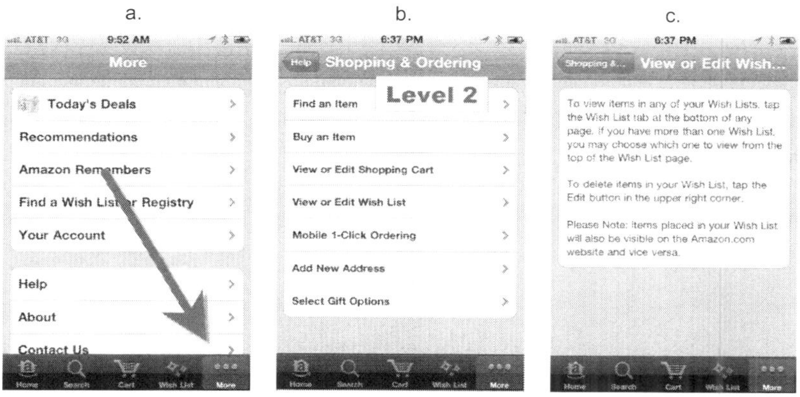

FAAwait, shown in Fig. 3.14, provides information about flight delays and airport closures. The icon in the top right corner (a.) links to a single page of Help. This contains a lengthy amount of prose. The information would have worked better with smaller snippets and a larger typeface.

A link at the bottom of the Help page (b.) goes to the main web page for the product. This page doesn't provide any Help info. However, the web site has a detailed FAQ page (c.). It might have been better to link directly to that page.

Fig. 3.14 FAAwait

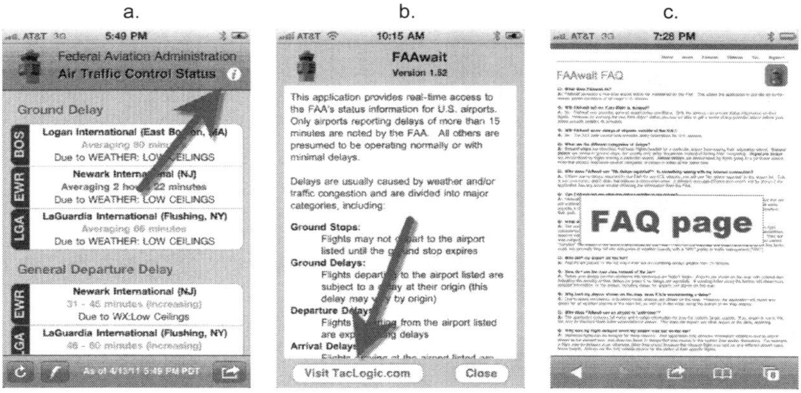

Videos and Demos

Many support situations can benefit from a richer level of presentation to the user. Videos and demos can provide a more engaging experience. The audio/visual capabilities of video make it a great choice for showing complex tasks and helping the viewer feel at ease. Demonstrations are useful for presenting an automated tutorial about tasks and procedures.

However, each form of UA has its trade-offs. Videos can take away control from the user. A video launch page should indicate the duration. The player should have controls for pausing, rewinding, and fast-forwarding. On the development side, video production can be very time-intensive. They also require programming resources to integrate them with the app. Videos can also be very expensive if you need to localize the content for other locales.

An earlier example (Fig. 3.4c) showed **eBay's** use of a popup and Help topics. Fig. 3.15 shows the link sequence leading to four instructional videos that are hosted by YouTube. The videos are well done and probably deserve a bit more prominence (a.) on the Help navigation page. It might help for the list of videos (b.) to match the style used on the Help navigation page. Clicking on the video thumbnail (c.) starts the YouTube player and the video. The video panel is linked to the app with a Back button.

Fig. 3.15 eBay videos

a. b. c.

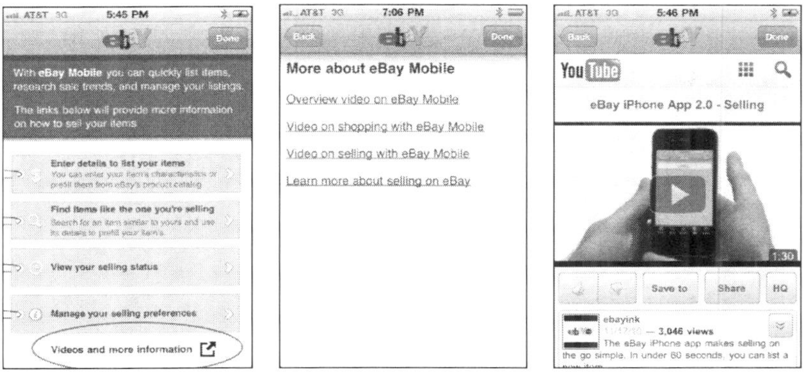

Convertbot is shown in Fig. 3.16. This app is a cousin to the Weightbot app described earlier. The first time you open the app a message box gives you the option of running a demo. This is a live demo. A wizard automatically guides you through the basic operation of the app. A series of pop-ups provide brief explanations. The demo can also be run from the Support page.

Fig. 3.16 Convertbot demo

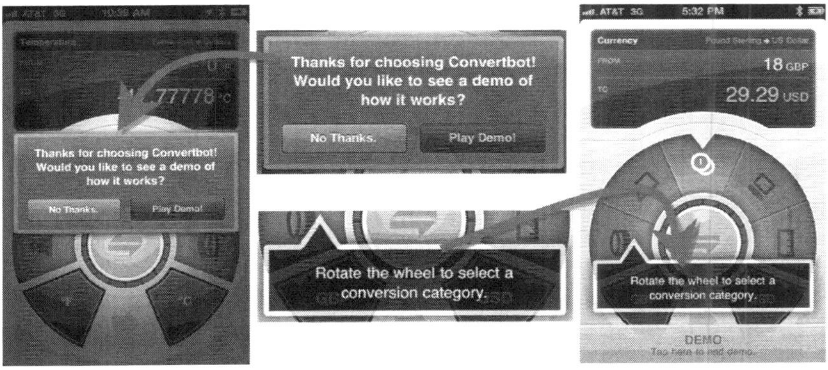

UA in Multiple Forms

Depending on the complexity of the app, it can helpful to have more than one form of user assistance. The apps in Fig. 3.17 take this approach. They were described in the previous sections.

In addition to highlighting the UI to first-time users, SoundHound has a Help panel. AutoCAD has a Help panel in addition to its guided help. Convertbot has a Help panel in addition to its automated demo. (The colors in the Convertbot image have been inverted. The actual panel uses white text on black.)

Fig. 3.17 Using more than one form of UA

SoundHound AutoCAD Convertbot

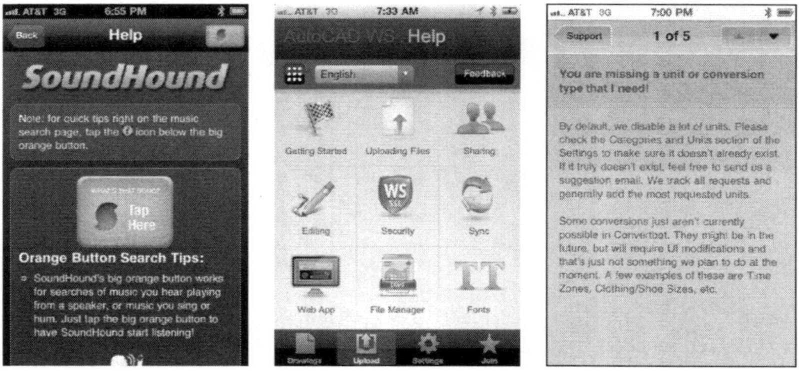

Google Search was mentioned earlier for its guided help. This app also has a link to Help information, but the way it is implemented is very unwieldy. The user has to go into Settings, tap "Help and Feedback," then tap "Help and Discussion." This process brings you to a web page where you then have to find your way to the Help Center. Once you get to that page, there is a lot of good information, however. The idea of having a link to web-based content is a good one. It would just be better if it were one-click away from the workspace.

Fig. 3.18 Google Help

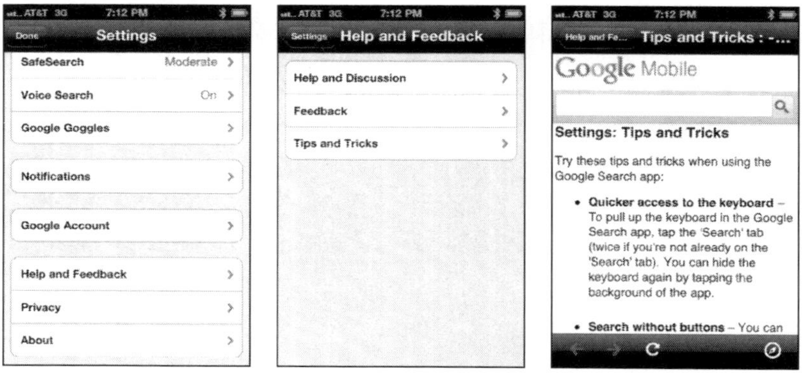

Take-away and Preview

Design in the mobile space is just as challenging as in other areas of software development. The examples in this section highlight the variety in app designs and the many forms of user assistance that are being employed. Your first important step toward your own design should be to evaluate existing designs to determine which approaches you think work and which don't. Be on the lookout for innovative ways to embed UA directly in the user assistance. Carefully consider the pros and cons of the potential solutions you and your team come up with. Build on what you know works with other forms of software, but be sensitive to the unique aspects of mobile.

The next chapter utilizes your design and populates it with the content that communicates with your users.

4 Creating Helpful Words and Images

How do people find their way through applications? Generally, words and images carry the weight when it comes to path-finding in software. It doesn't matter whether it is an enterprise-level desktop application, a consumer web site, or a mobile app. Text and graphics direct the user in performing tasks. Usually, however, users don't ignore the text and images in early interactions with the app.

Unfortunately, the text in the user interface or the Help section of an app is often created with little or no thought. It is very likely that the labels you see in an app are using the words that first came to mind when a developer assembled the first draft of a page in an app. That is not an ideal situation. With the smaller screen real estate of mobile devices, apps are limited to fewer words and smaller images. It is more important than ever to find the perfect content to fill that valuable space.

The Language of Gestures

The previous chapter on design showed many different ways to add user assistance to an app. Some of those involve adding elements directly into the user interface. Individual word choices are extremely important and it is worth testing them with users to find the best words. Your word choices may change depending on the mobile platform you intend to support.

A great book about this subject is *Language and Communication: Essential Concepts for User Interface and Documentation Design* (ISBN-13: 978-0195108385). It was written by Agnes Kukulska-Hulme and is based on her academic research in this area. The book is over ten years old but the information is still relevant, especially for mobile UI text. A general theme is the importance of evaluating language at a very granular level – examining individual word choices.

There are several types of gestures used in working with mobile apps. These gestures have added a new vocabulary for user assistance professionals to absorb and use. *Clicks* have been replaced with *taps*. *Scrolling* has been replaced with *flicks*.

When putting together UA we need to be aware of these gestures, understand where they apply, and present them to our users in the appropriate way. The touch gestures that make up the bulk of interactions are shown in Table 1.

Table 1 Common touch gestures

Gesture	Action
Tap	Similar to a click
Double-tap	Similar to a double click
Flick	A quick vertical or horizontal movement to change the current view
Touch and Hold	Pressing without releasing until an event occurs
Pinch Open, **Pinch Close (iOS)** **Pinch (Android)** **Stretch, Pinch (WP7)**	A multi-touch gesture to increase/decrease the size of the contents of the current view
Type/Enter	Using the keyboard to enter text
Select	A general reference to tapping on a specific item in a list

The first four items in Table 1 are common to iOS, Android, and WP7. That makes life a bit easier for UI text.

Tap and **Double-tap** are straightforward and analogous to clicks.

Flick is a new entity for user assistance. It may not be a term that most users are familiar with but it is reasonably self-explanatory. However, different apps may employ flicks in different ways.

The **Pinch** gesture has subtle platform differences. If you support two or three of those platforms, the most accurate approach would be to use the respective terms. However, that can be unwieldy and you might want to standardize on one term. This would need to be addressed in your cross-platform strategy.

The list in Table 1 is just a portion of the overall gestures used in mobile. There are other gestures that address less common interactions. For example, in iOS there is a **Shake**. In iOS and Android there is a **Swipe**. There is a **Pan** in WP7 and a **Drag** in Android.

Type and **Select** are not terms that are defined in the SDKs of the various platforms. However, they are very common actions and should be included in any list.

Using gesture language for UA

The previous chapter discussed a number of real-world apps in terms of their user assistance designs. If you look more closely at them, you can see their terminology choices for commands. The examples in Fig. 4.1 show how terms were used in explanations to first-time users and in guided help. ToonPAINT introduces tapping with a very descriptive graphic. Weightbot illustrates the rotation of the device needed to change the information display. AutoCADuses gesture terms in its guided Help.

Fig. 4.1

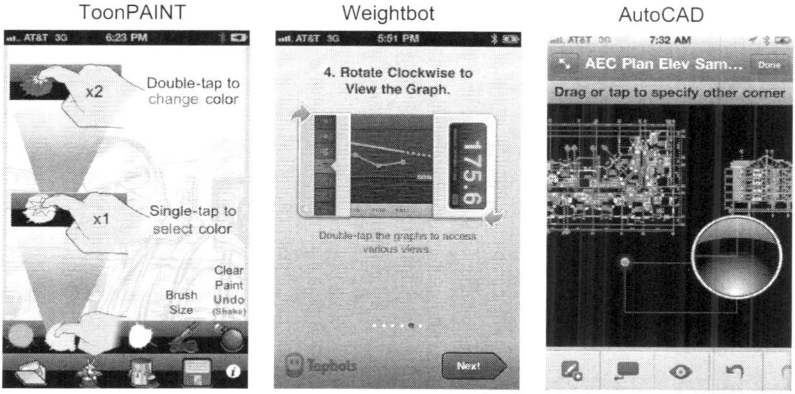

The apps in Fig. 4.2 described touch terminology in several different situations. Notice that Convertbot used the word *Press* to activate the OK button. In iOS, the official term would be *Tap*. Is the use of Press wrong? A better question is whether Press accomplishes the goal in communicating to the user. Your own analysis and usability testing will help define a style guide that fits the needs of your apps. Once you have that in place you can maintain consistency across an app or line of apps.

Calvetica used gesture terminology in a FAQ. The explanation of gestures for eBay was done as a narrated script in a video.

Fig. 4.2

Gesture resources

Designer Luke Wroblewski and his colleagues have put together a very comprehensive review of touch gestures for many platforms. This guide is a great resource and will save you time so you don't have to dig this information out of the platform documentation. The guide also provides links to the user interface guidelines for the various platforms.

- *Touch Gesture Reference Guide*:
  http://www.lukew.com/ff/entry.asp?1071

Fig. 4.3 Excerpt from the *Touch Gesture Reference Guide*

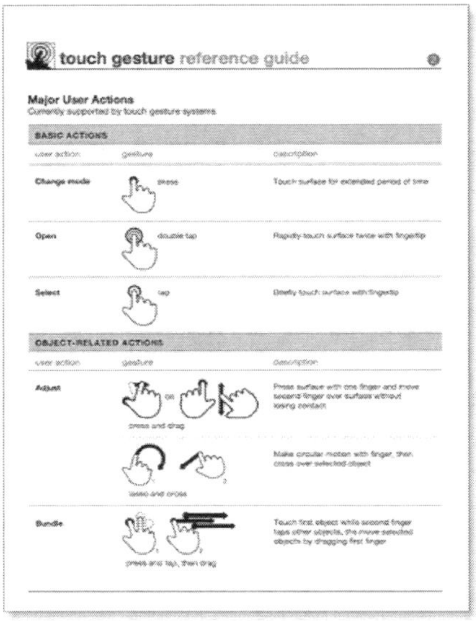

Simon Whatley, a prolific blogger about web design, has pulled together a comprehensive list of UI guidelines published by the various mobile platforms.

- User Interface Guidelines for Mobile and Tablet Devices:
  http://www.simonwhatley.co.uk/user-interface-guidelines-for-mobile-and-tablet-devices

Translation issues for gesture terms

The impact of gestures on UA was described earlier in this chapter. There is a whole new vocabulary of taps and flicks that we need to become familiar with. That becomes even more involved if we have to support translations of our content. The language of gestures is new to translators as well. The nuances of translating gestures will be a challenge.

Useful examples of gesture translation can be found in the Apple user guides. Apple provides a list of all of its manuals in each of the supported languages.

- Apple list of manuals:
  http://www.apple.com/support/country/?dest=manuals

Table 2 is a comparison of gesture terms from the iPhone User Guide in English and Spanish.

Table 2 Comparison of languages in iPhone User Guide

English	Spanish
Tap	Pulse *
Double tap	Pulce dos veces
Touch and hold	Mantenga Pulsado **
Flick	Deslice el dedo ***
Drag	Arrastre
Pinch	Pellizco
Shake	Agite

* In English, there is a distinction between Tap and Press. Press is used when referring to the mechanical "Home" button on the iPhone. However, in Spanish, Pulse is used for both Tap and Press.

** There are at least three variants in the Spanish version of the User Guide for "Touch and hold." A literal English translation of "Mantenga Pulsado" is "keep pressing."

*** For Flick, the iPhone User Guide uses the literal translation of "slide your finger." It is usually modified with "hacia la izquierda o hacia la derecha" ("left or right"). In another passage they use "Pulse ligeramente" for "Flick." The literal translation is "Press lightly."

These are just some of the variants in English/Spanish. The translation companies face a major challenge in developing a library of standard gesture terminology.

Using Language in UI Elements

There are many parts of a mobile app where text is employed. Ideally, a UA professional should vet all of these elements. It helps to become familiar with the names of the various elements so you can communicate well with your team members. The best way to do that is by digging into the editing tools for the respective platforms.

While the platforms share many similar elements, they almost all have platform-specific names. If you have access to the project code, you can experiment with text changes by adjusting the attributes of the elements. This is discussed in separate chapters for each of the major platforms.

Table 3 shows some of the common UI element names and where to find them.

Table 3 Platform-specific user interface elements

Platform	Location	Types of UI Elements
iOS	Inspector	Button, Label, Text Field, Segmented Control, Tab Bar
Android	Form Widgets	TextView, Button, CheckBox, ToggleButton, Radio Button
Windows Phone 7	ToolBox	Text box, Button, Hyperlink button, Radio button, Text block, List box

Case Study — Timewerks

WritersUA provided guidance for the Timewerks app produced by Sorth LLC. The app provides a quick and easy way for contractors and consultants to keep track of project time and be able to invoice clients. One of the keys features of the app is the Task Timer, shown in Fig. 4.4. The timer is essentially a stopwatch for collecting the time spent on a particular task. When a task is complete, the time duration can be assigned directly to the associated project.

The user can continue to work with other parts of the app while the timer is in action. However, the original button label to move away from this screen was *Dismiss*. That word can communicate a false impression of what will happen when you tap it. A user may be hesitant to tap it if they think they will lose the recorded time.

Fig. 4.4 Start Finish Mock-up

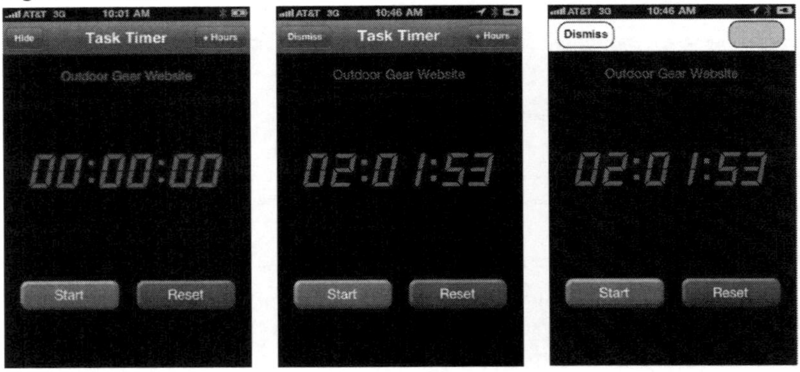

During usability testing, we used a simple card sort test with mockups of the page. There were four variations of the text used for the button in the top left corner: Dismiss, Back, Hide, and Done. We established the scenario and put the mockup options in front of the test subjects. *Hide* received the most positive response. There was a tie for *Back* and *Done*. *Dismiss* brought up the rear.

Factors that affect user choices in a usability test are the number of options offered and the quality of those options. The number of options will depend on resources and the level of testing integrity you want to achieve. The quality of the options requires some study and understanding of words. A thesaurus can offer up ideas. However, not all good choices are necessarily synonyms.

The test in this case study could have been more refined if the mockups had been done through the iOS simulator. This requires access to the source code. The use of simulators is described in the chapters on iOS, Android, and WP7.

Case Study — Quickoffice

WritersUA provided guidance for the Quickoffice app. This app offers a mobile suite of productivity tools including a word processor and spreadsheet. In this case, there were several menu items with terms that were problematic.

As shown in Fig. 4.5 one of the Quickword menus used the word *Font*. This is a word that many consumers are not familiar with. Using *Text* as a replacement makes it clear that the color changes the text. Technically "text" is not synonymous with "font." When you are limited to one or two words due to space, you sometimes need to make these kinds of decisions.

Fig. 4.5 Quickword

The Font/Text choice was also used in the Quicksheet menu, shown in Fig. 4.6. A separate issue was the term *Cell background*. *Cell* is another term that may not be familiar to a lot of users. These users might be clicking on a cell without knowing what it is called. What the feature does is change the background color so we used that as the label.

Fig. 4.6 Quicksheet

With this project, we had access to the application code through a provisioning file. A provisioning file enables a test version of an app. Ironically, that wasn't helpful for this task. Quickoffice uses a custom menu structure that does not work with the iOS simulator. In this situation, testing needs to be done through mock-ups.

It can be easy to dismiss these kinds of wording changes as minor and not worth the effort to consider and test. The case to make when pitching this kind of work is to consider the opportunity cost of not taking the time to fine-tune every aspect of an app. Unlike the desktop application market, the mobile app stores are filled with hundreds of thousands of apps competing for visibility. Most product categories offer dozens of similar apps. Little touches can be the difference between retaining customers or not; between getting three stars in a review versus four or five.

For interaction with "hard" buttons, using *tap* may not be appropriate. Apple's iPhone User Guide uses *Press* when talking about the Home button. With Android devices, defining buttons becomes a difficult task. Fig. 4.7 is a collage of button bars from a variety of phones running Android. The different looks, placement, and names for these buttons creates a real challenge when it comes to writing instructions. The Sony Xperia Play, shown in Fig. 4.8, uses a gaming scheme for the device controls. This is an unfamiliar format to anyone but seasoned gamers and will require UA attention.

Fig. 4.7 Gallery of Android button bars
(Engadget.com, used with permission)

Fig. 4.8 Sony Xperia Play

Writing Procedures

Chapter 3 (page 23) presented a number of examples where detailed procedures were hosted in the Help section of an app. While this type of UA looks a lot like what we might see on the desktop, when you get into the details of the designs you find a lot of differences.

Brevity continues to be central to any design. The minimal screen real estate can't support large amounts of text and graphics without extensive gesturing by the users. Using small font sizes just makes the information unreadable unless the user pinches and stretches the text. The placement and formatting of content is as important as the writing of the words.

Navigation is difficult for mobile users. Two levels of menus plus a level for topics is the maximum you would want to use. Even that requires the user to do a lot of navigation.

The wildly different UIs that we find in our apps mean that users can't necessarily carry conventions from one app to another. Unique icons, buttons, and menu structures can create angst for users.

This section uses several case studies to highlight challenges and solutions in dealing with procedure development.

Case Study — TimeWerks Quick Start Tutorial

One of the interesting aspects of working with mobile UA is that you may find yourself using techniques that are seldom used in today's desktop UA. Some examples can be found in the Timewerks Quick Start Tutorial (Fig. 4.9) created by WritersUA. The tutorial takes up just over one windowful of content. Fig. 4.9a shows the entire topic in one long strip.

Color: Any text that applies to menu or button text was colored a shade of red (Fig. 4.9b.) This makes it easy to follow the succession of UI interactions without necessarily reading all of the words.

Fig. 4.9 Timewerks Quick Start tutorial (extended view showing the entire topic)

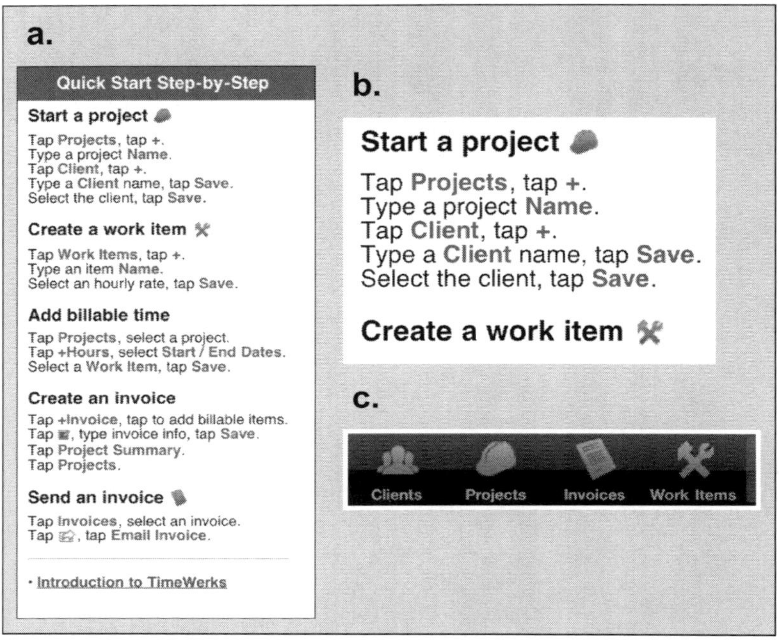

Steps: Apps frequently have interactions that are two closely related steps: a tap and a tap, a tap and a select, a tap and type. These "half-steps" can be combined into a single step. For example (b.), "Tap **Work Items**, tap **+**." Using a shorthand notation for these mini-procedures saves a lot of room.

You can make a good case that conjunctive adverbs like "then" and conjunctions like "and" can be sacrificed in the name of space. It depends on how critical those words are in getting the point across. Some writers may feel that "then" is important enough to always include. Another possible option is to use an arrow (→).

Icons: Each section of the tutorial includes the icon that matches the related icon in the Tab bar (Fig. 4.9c). This helps orient the user as to what words connect with what item. The icon images are based on the images used in the build of the app. The icon images were adjusted to be slightly smaller than the icons in the Tab bar. This saved a surprising amount of vertical and horizontal space in the topic.

Numbering: Most mobile apps support the ability to use HTML ordered list markup for numbering of steps. It is also possible to just type in the numbers as text. However, using numbers takes up a surprising amount of horizontal space. A lengthy line means it may break to a second line, thereby taking up vertical space. Because of this issue, the

QuickStart tutorial doesn't use numbered steps. If space is still an issue, you might consider grouping numbered steps into a single, continuous paragraph. For example:

> **To Copy an Image:** 1. Tap Xxxxxx. 2. Double tap the Xxxxx on the xxx. 3. Select Xxxxx.

Periods: Another consideration is the use of periods at the end of sentences in procedures. This is less about saving space than having an appropriate look and feel to your text. Periods are left out more than not in mobile documentation. This subtle lack of formalness seems to fit the mobile sensibility. The QuickStart Tutorial omits periods but you could easily make an argument to leave them in.

Case Study — Apple iPhone User Guide

Apple provides a comprehensive browser-based user guide in support of the iPhone. Since Apple is the keeper of the flame for iOS standards, it can be useful to look at how they put together their own Help topics. The guide, shown in Fig. 4.10a., covers the basics of using the iPhone as well as documenting the apps that ship with the device.

Fig. 4.10b is a page with several procedures for working with the Weather app. The primary procedure of adding cities to a list uses the task-oriented title of "Add a city." This is followed by three lines of numbered steps. UI icons are used where applicable. Secondary tasks use a single paragraph rather than separate numbered steps. Boldface is used to highlight the task titles.

Fig. 4.10c is from the Camera app. This app uses a set of non-standard UI controls. A sample image is placed in the procedure with call-outs to the various controls. The graphic does a good job of quickly mapping out the controls. Unfortunately, the typeface is small and the image can't be stretched larger.

Fig. 4.10 a b c

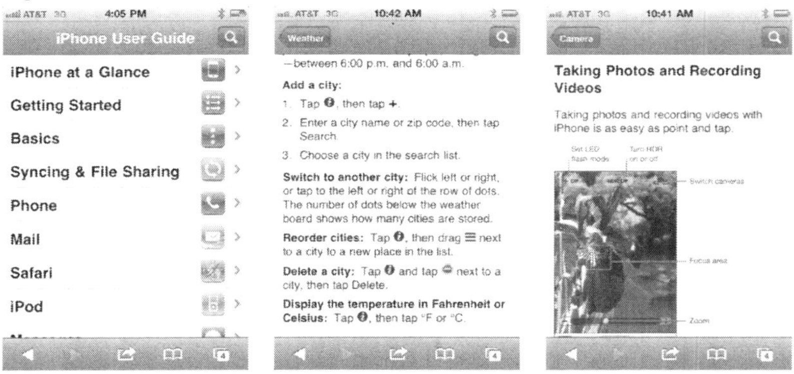

Fig. 4.10d is from the section on iPhone Basics. Descriptive graphics are used to demonstrate finger gestures. It is likely that as gestures become familiar to most people, this type of Help won't need to be provided. However, there are a lot of new gesture interactions appearing in apps every day. It may continue to be an area of need.

There are a few elements of this Help that aren't too useful. One is the use of dialog box screen captures in some topics as shown in Fig. 4.10e. If a screen capture is really justified it should probably be a larger, *partial* capture of the relevant area. Another dubious element is shown in Fig. 4.10f.: The reminder about needing iTunes is supplemented with a link to the iTunes web site. However, the procedure is limited to using iTunes on Mac OS X. The link really can't help the user.

The presentation of the user guide topics is fairly consistent. There must have been either a tool-based or paper-based style guide in use.

Fig. 4.10 **d** **e** **f**

The Help system itself is stitched together with a complicated jumble of HTML and JavaScript that is referred to behind the scenes as "pastrykit." This is discussed in the Browser-based Help section, page 64. However, the bottom line is that the code for building a similar Help system is not available to developers outside of Apple.

More examples

Here are a few more examples showing different approaches to language in procedures.

PhotoPad, in Fig. 4.11, has a quick start page (a.) for first-time users. It uses task-oriented action verbs rather than gesture language. However, the Help pages (b.) use the gesture language when it gets more specific. The Color Selection page (c.) describes an interaction that is unique to this app. It requires a double-tap with the second tap being held down. This is a difficult concept to explain. We are likely to see many unique gesture interactions appearing in the software we support.

Fig. 4.11 PhotoPad

a. b. c.

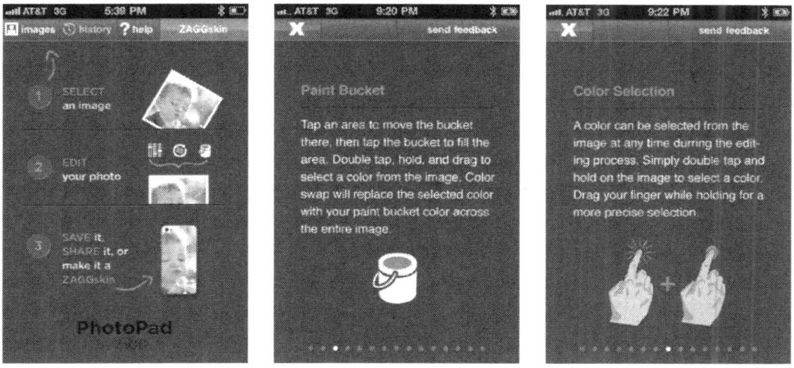

In Fig. 4.12, Fantasia Paint uses an elaborate call-out page for first time users. For Office OneNote, the getting-started topic uses colored headings and bold for user interface elements. The Photo Collage page uses "Select" rather than "Tap" for selecting a radio button. It also uses "Slide" instead of "Flick." The preferences page for Tasks Anywhere uses a lower case "p" for the "preferences" title. This is somewhat common in the Windows Phone "Metro" design look and feel. It also uses a font size that is extremely small.

(Note: The images in Fig. 4.12 are photos of a WP7 device. WP7 does not provide a way to capture screen images without source code, even with the emulator.)

Fig. 4.12

Fantasia Paint

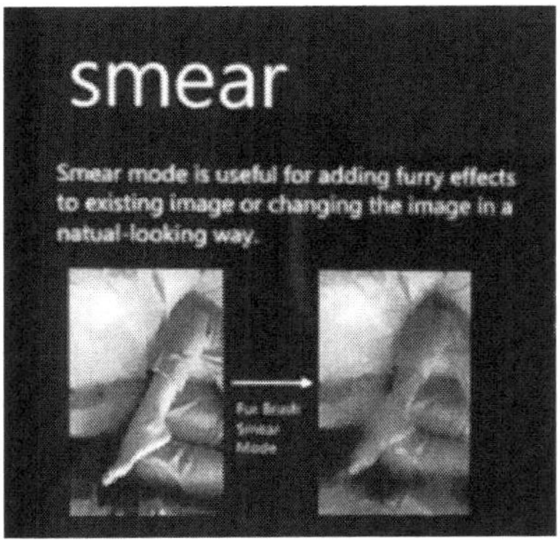

Office Word

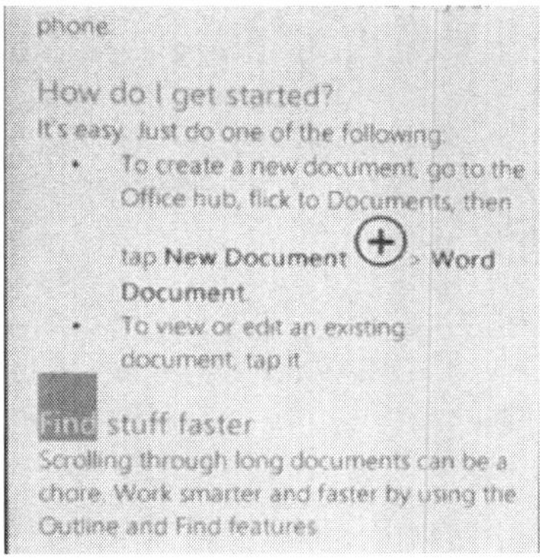

Photo Collage

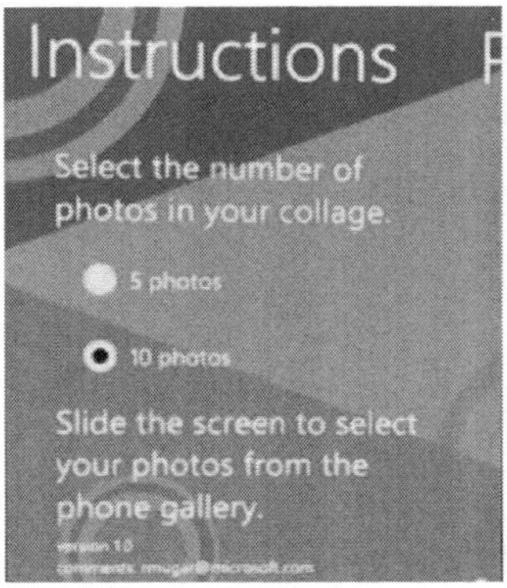

Tasks Anywhere

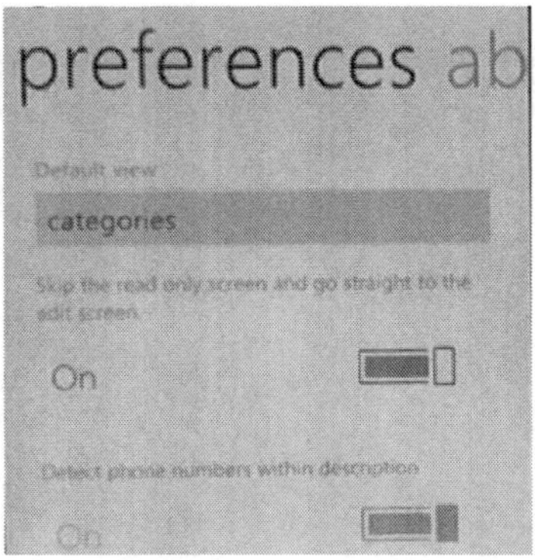

The following article from Jakob Nielsen summarizes research from R.I. Singh at the University of Alberta. The researchers found that comprehension scores for online reading on mobile devices were half those for desktop reading. The minimal screen real estate limited how much information the reader could see. This in turn means the reader must divert their attention and spend the time to manipulate the content within the screen frame.

- Mobile Content is Twice as Difficult:: http://www.useit.com/alertbox/mobile-content-comprehension.html

Messaging

Messaging within an app is another method of providing user assistance. Message screens are designed to appear in response to certain user interface selections or events in the apps. Often these pop-ups are used to present "Error" messages. In these cases, it is better to phrase the message in a positive way rather than as a reprimand to the user. Messages can also be used to provide proactive Help.

A typical message box consists of a message title, the message, and a label for a button to dismiss the message. Generally, message boxes are enabled through programming code. Your team will need to decide whether you will edit the message text yourself or communicate the changes to a developer. This form of UI text can be more difficult to work with than the elements described earlier in Table 3.

Every platform has its own way(s) of presenting messages. Fig. 4.13 shows messages in three different platforms. There are varying rules for size, formatting, and the use of graphics.

Fig. 4.13 Message text for different platforms

a. iPhone b. Android c. WP7

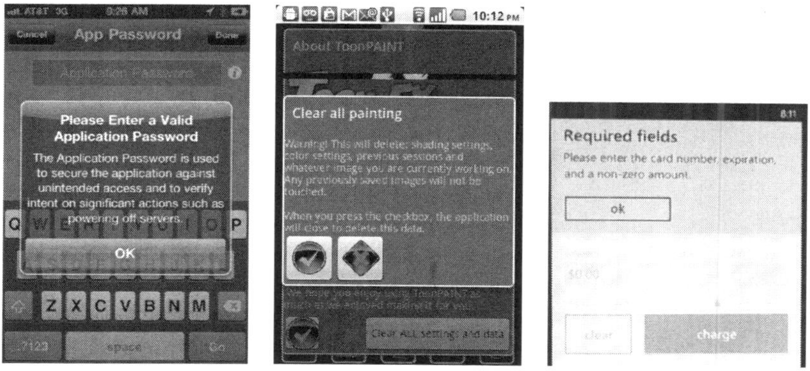

You may find user interface text used in unusual settings. Fig. 4.14 shows UI text being used in an opaque button bar being used with the device camera.

Fig. 4.14 Help text used in an opaque UI element

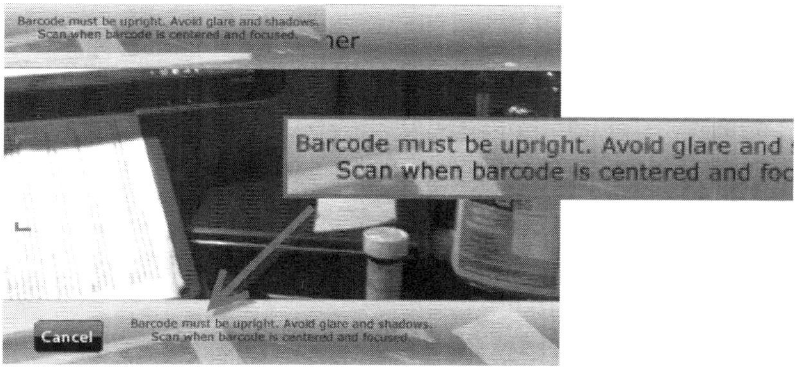

Video Tutorials

Using videos for software instruction is a growing trend. The most interesting videos tend to be ones that use a variety of media and different scenes. Limiting the video to a single-shot view of the screen is a good way to lose the attention of your viewers. The best videos are fast-paced, visually arresting, and to the point for today's mobile users.

Instructional video is a very involved topic. If you are interested in this medium there are hundreds of books and web resources devoted to all aspects of it. The following items provide a brief introduction to this discipline. Fig. 4.15 shows a summary of the components typically used with instructional video in support of software.

Fig. 4.15 Instructional video components

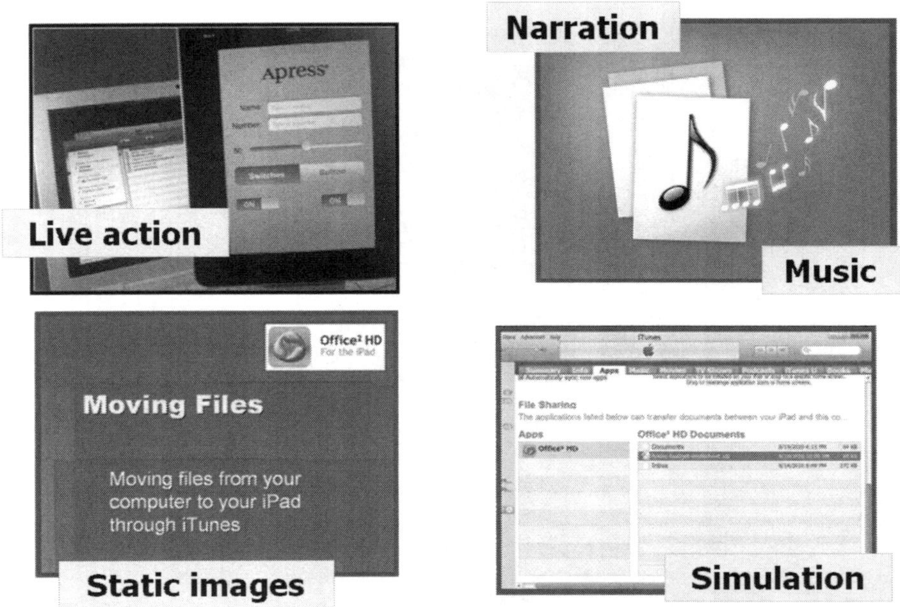

Live action: A trend in instructional video is to use live action. This gives video a real-world feel. You see someone actually completing the steps with the software. The availability of inexpensive, high-resolution video cameras makes the investment in equipment minimal. One of the downsides is the need to pay close attention to lighting and camerawork and have a pair of hands ready for modeling. The apps from eBay and AutoCAD both use live video segments, as shown in Fig. 4.16.

Fig. 4.16

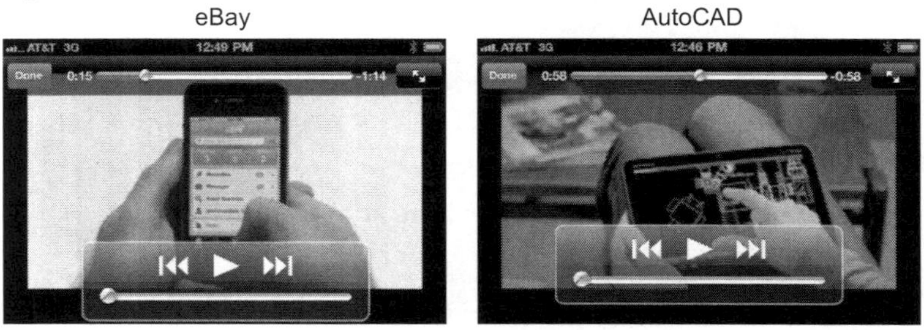

Simulation: There are many options for screen capture software. Tools like Camtasia and Captivate offer a relatively low-priced set of tools for recording a series of interactions with software. You can edit your recordings to highlight and zoom in on specific sections of the screen and to add special effects and call-outs. However, lengthy recordings can be very boring if they aren't supplemented with other types of media.

Narration can add a lot of interest to a video. In the past, this has required a professional narrator. The more recent trend is toward a more informal YouTube style. Even amateurs can do an acceptable job with a bit of practice and a good microphone.

The alternative to narration is to embed captions and/or provide a transcript with the video. Either approach creates a dilemma for translation.

Music can help set a mood and create interest. Many services offer licensed musical loops at very low prices. The iStockPhoto service has hundreds of tunes in its library that are available for $20-30, including a license to use it in deliverables. Almost every video can benefit from music at the beginning and end. Using music in the middle is acceptable but less common. The same software used for capturing and editing video will generally have controls for embedding music with fade-in/out.

Static images: A video will usually use a number of static images. These include title slides with logos, step summaries for procedures, flowcharts, photos, and screen captures. A good editing suite will make it easy to integrate these static images with your live action, simulation, music, and narration. A static image can be given a duration so that it remains on screen as long as necessary. Slides can be produced in PowerPoint, grabbed with a screen capture utility, and then embedded in the video.

The best way to work with the media elements described above is with a video editing suite. You can purchase perfectly capable editing tools for $75-$150. For You Tube-style instructional videos there really is no need to spend more. An editing tool lets you import video clips, has trimming tools for setting the beginning and end of the clips, and allows you to add a variety of transitions between the clips. Parallel tracks along a timeline allow for music, narration, captions, and special effects.

When working with video it is always good to have a computer with fast graphics processing, a fast hard drive, a lot of memory, and as much storage space as you can afford.

If you are doing live shots, you will need a camera and a lighting kit. For sound, you'll need a good microphone and possibly sound mixing software. A graphics editor and screen capture utility are needed for working with static images.

Image Formats

The formats used for images in mobile are the same cast of characters we have for web development. The two most common formats are PNG and JPG. Generally, PNG is the best format for illustrations – while JPG is best suited to photos. Both of these formats have particularly good compression schemes and leave a small footprint. The format used in iOS apps is almost exclusively PNG.

One of the main challenges for graphic designers is creating images that work well across platforms. Mobile devices come in a wide array of screen dimensions and resolutions. And the number of options in mobile screens continues to increase. The difference in how an image looks in one platform versus another is often undetectable to the user. In other cases, it can be a problem. There is a lot of useful information in the following WP7 article.

- Image format considerations: http://windowsphone.interoperabilitybridges.com/articles/chapter-5-image-format-considerations-in-migration-of-iphone-applications-to-windows-phone-7

- Designing for iPhone 4's Retina Display:
  A description of why and how to take advantage of automatic pixel doubling in iOS 4.
  http://globalmoxie.com/blog/designing-for-iphone4-retina-display.shtml

Take-away and Preview

Mobile apps have introduced users to the language of gestures – a new way for interacting with software. This presents user assistance professionals with an interesting challenge. Helping users in working with our apps means we may also have to assist them in understanding how to control the user interface with their fingers.

The variations in gesture language between platforms makes our jobs even more difficult. We need to anticipate what a user knows already and integrate those assumptions with our own designs. Usability testing can provide us with data to bolster our confidence in our designs.

Due to the limited screen real estate on mobile devices, the words and images we use need to be extremely efficient. Word choices, image placement, and overall presentation of our content are keys to an effective UA solution.

The next several chapters delve into the details of user assistance implementation in a variety of forms and for a variety of platforms and devices.

5 Browser-based Help

A common method of providing user assistance is by using browser-based Help pages. In fact, this has become the dominant method of delivering Help in support of desktop applications. Using open standard markup such as HTML, XML, and CSS provides a good single-source, cross-browser delivery solution.

It wasn't always that way. The browser wars of a decade ago made it difficult to get consistent presentation of information. Even today, there are still gaps in browser support and browser versions leapfrog each other in features.

The wars may be in the past but browser incompatibility has moved into the mobile space. Mobile browsers are all over the place in terms of what they support and how. Android, WP7, and iOS all have different browsers. Couple that with the fact that even within a single manufacturer the desktop and mobile browsers support different feature sets. Microsoft's Internet Explorer is different on the desktop than it is on WP7. The same goes for Apple and Google.

Browser Compatibility

On the desktop, it has become easy to use your browser of choice. You download the browser you want and assign it to be your default. Mobile is more restrictive. First of all the native apps are automatically linked to the default browser of the platform. You can download another browser but you can't easily make it the system default.

What this means for UA professionals is a lot of hard work. Our browser-based solutions need to be tested for each of the platforms that we support. Mobile browsers are likely to support different versions of HMTL and CSS than their desktop counterparts. Given the rapidly growing number of devices, it is more important than ever to stick to standard markup. It is also important to have at least one or two devices for each of the platforms (iOS, Android, and so on) that your app supports for testing purposes.

A nice testing tool has been developed by Niels Leenheer, a browser blogger. The tool consists of "The HTML5 Test" web page. When you load the page in a browser, the tool gives you a numerical score as shown in Fig. 5.1. The higher the score the better the browser is in supporting full HTML 5 functionality. In addition to the raw score, you get a breakdown of the scoring. The results from several browsers are shown in Table 4.

This table is just a snapshot in time. You are likely to find different numbers if you test the most current versions of these browsers.

- The HTML5 Test:
  http://html5test.com/

Table 4 Browser compatibility with HTML5

Browser	Score
Chrome 10 (desktop)	288
Blackberry Playbook	258
Safari 5 (desktop)	228
iOS 4.3 (Safari mobile)	206
Android FroYo 2.2	182
Firefox 3.6 (desktop)	155
IE 9 beta (desktop)	130
IE in WP7	17

Fig. 5.1 Mobile Safari test

Microsoft is definitely the laggard in HTML5 support. The score for IE 9 was low and IE 8 was worse. The score for the WP7 browser was bottom of the barrel. Somewhat surprisingly, the relatively new Blackberry Playbook had the best score among mobile browsers.

Designing a Help Template

Viewing HTML content is easier for the user when you take the time to optimize the page layout, line spacing, text fonts, and colors. One way to do this is by iteratively changing a prototype page until you get just the right balance. A Cascading Style Sheet (CSS) is the key to doing this. Your HTML files contain the content and style elements. A CSS file contains the definitions of the various styles. By making changes to the style sheet, you can instantly change the look of the content.

The tools for designing your browser-based Help can be as simple as a text editor, a desktop browser, and a mobile device. The venerable text editor is plenty capable of creating markup for smartphone-sized Help. A basic procedure topic is probably only going to be in the range of 2-5 KB in size. This is assuming the use of a cascading style sheet for formatting and a topic length that fits within one screen without scrolling.

Case Study – Timewerks

The Timewerks product was discussed in Chapter 3. The language guidelines used for the Quick Start tutorial, shown in Fig. 5.2a, were discussed there as well.

The Quick Start content was rendered for browsing using HTML and CSS. The Quick Start procedure is stored on a server and called by the mobile app. The content is inserted into the app with a web view control (Fig. 5.2b). Different platforms have different names for this kind of view. In iOS, it is implemented with "UIWebView."

Fig. 5.2 Timewerks Quick Start tutorial

a. b.

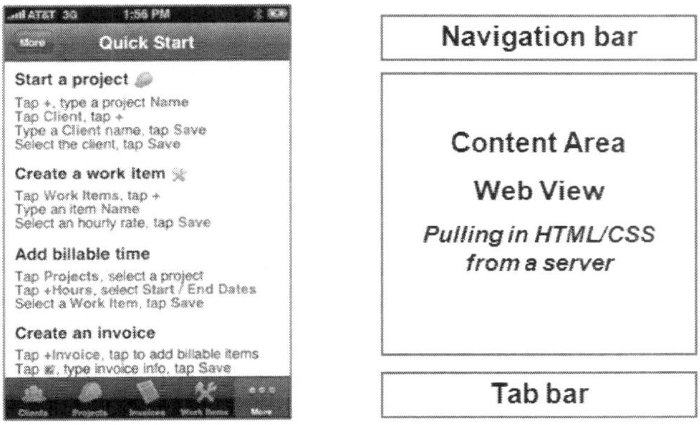

The typeface, colors, and spacing were defined using a number of styles, as shown in Fig. 5.3. The HTML, CSS, and icon image files were all posted to a server.

Fig. 5.3 Timewerks CSS style sheet

```
<style TYPE="text/css">

    p.titlebar { background: #993300;
                 color: white;
                                    font-weight: bold;
                                    font-size: 14pt;
                                    line-height: 200%;
                                    font-family: helvetica, arial,
sans-serif;
                                    text-indent: 2em;
                                    margin-bottom: -.25em }

          p.step    { color: black;
                                    font-weight: normal;
                                    font-size: 12pt;
                                    line-height: 100%;
                                    font-family: helvetica, arial,
sans-serif }

    p.heading  { color: black;
                                    font-weight: bold;
                                    font-size: 12pt;
                                    line-height: 100%;
                                    font-family: helvetica, arial,
sans-serif;
                                    margin-bottom: -.5em }

    em              { color: #993300;
                                    font-weight: bold;
                                    font-size: 12pt;
                                    font-style: normal;
                                    font-family: helvetica, arial,
sans-serif }

  </style>
```

The Viewport <meta> tag

An important development in mobile browsing has been the Viewport <meta> tag. This tag will automatically scale your web content for optimal mobile viewing. One line of code in the <head> section of your HTML file is all that is needed to enable this behavior, as shown in Fig. 5.4.

Fig. 5.4 A basic Viewport tag

```
<head>
        <title>Introduction to Timewerks</title>
        <meta name="viewport" content="width=device-width" />
```

You can see the effect of this tag in Fig. 5.5. The page on the left is a standard web page being viewed in a mobile browser. The page on the right is what it looks like when the

Viewport tag is included. The mobile browser automatically adjusts the size of the content to fit the available screen real estate. It takes the width of the HTML page and expands it to be as wide as possible within the browser window. The rest of the content scales vertically downward in proportion.

Fig. 5.5 Comparison without (left) and with (right) the use of the Viewport tag

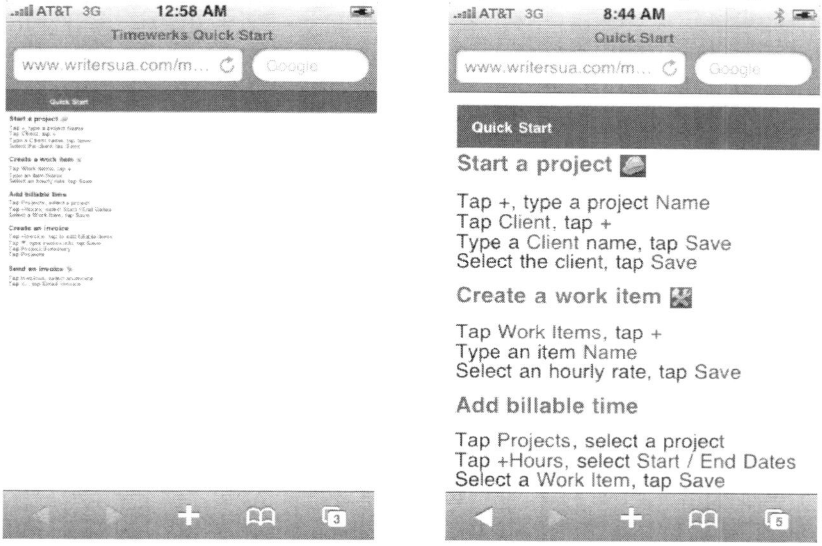

You can see this effect for yourself by viewing the following URL in your desktop and mobile browsers.

- Timewerks Quick Start prototype: www.writersua.com/mobile/timewerks/qs.htm

Apple originally created this tag and supports it in its Safari mobile browser. It has been copied by most of the other mobile browser developers.

That's the quick and easy look at the Viewport tag. There are a lot of design options available that can get pretty involved. There are also considerations unique to the various platforms. The following articles provide good guidance.

- Safari Web Content Guide - Configuring the Viewport: http://developer.apple.com/library/safari/#documentation/AppleApplications/Reference/SafariWebContent/UsingtheViewport/UsingtheViewport.html#//apple_ref/doc/uid/TP40006509-SW1

- WP7 Viewport: http://blogs.msdn.com/b/iemobile/archive/2010/11/22/the-ie-mobile-viewport-on-windows-phone-7.aspx http://blogs.msdn.com/b/iemobile/archive/2011/01/21/managing-the-browser-viewport-in-windows-phone-7.aspx

- The Viewport Metatag tutorial: http://davidbcalhoun.com/2010/viewport-metatag

- Metatags in HTML5:
  http://www.html-5.com/metatags/#meta-viewport

The Viewport tag is not part of the specifications put forward by the World Wide Web Consortium (W3C) and other organizations. Some browsers may not support this tag. If you're not sure, you'll need to test. If a browser doesn't support it, you will see a very small version of your page as shown in Fig. 5.5. The Viewport tag won't cause an error because the tag will just be ignored. If you need to support a browser that doesn't recognize Viewport, you may want to use the CSS media query and create different style sheets for the different browsers.

- Media Queries documentation from the World Web Web Consortium
  http://www.w3.org/TR/css3-mediaqueries/

- Article about implementing media queries for mobile use:
  http://shaunmackey.com/articles/mobile/using-media-query-to-declare-css-for-iphone/

A sample design process

The following iterative procedure was used in designing the Quick Start tutorial for the Timewerks iPhone app. It requires a desktop computer, an HTML/CSS editor, an FTP program, and a mobile device.

1) Create a sample topic in a standard HTML file.

   Include typical content including task headings, steps, and icons.

2) Create a style sheet.

   Start by identifying the various style elements in your topic page. This includes color, spacing, and typeface. You may want different styles for different elements of the topic.

   Next use the CSS specification to create a CSS file. Reference the CSS file in your HTML sample topic file. Place your HTML and CSS files in the same folder.

3) Review the sample topic.

   Use any standard desktop browser to view the content. Make adjustments as needed for style consistency and a nice look. Don't worry about the size of the text at this point.

4) Add the Viewport tag.

   As described in the previous section, the Viewport meta tag instructs the mobile browser to automatically scale the elements on the page. You won't see an effect in the desktop browser.

5) Post your sample topic to a server and view it in a mobile browser.

   It doesn't matter where you post your sample topic file as long as long as it is on a public-facing server. It helps to create a special folder since you will be making a lot of changes to your sample files. Type the URL of the sample topic file into your mobile browser and display the page. You may want to bookmark the page.

6) Adjust the settings as needed in your CSS and post the updated file.

   Based on what you see in the mobile browser, you are probably going to want to adjust the line spacing and font sizes. A rule of thumb is to size the elements so they are easily readable from a typical seated position in front of your desktop screen. In the Timewerks example, the point size for the title bar is 14 and the steps are 12pt.

7) Repeat Steps 5 and 6 until the topic page has the desired look when viewed through the mobile browser.

   Don't forget to refresh the page display in your browsers as you make your changes.

   You may want to review your sample using several of the mobile devices you are targeting.

Now that you have your style sheet in order, you can start creating the rest of your topic pages. Reference the same CSS file in all of the related pages.

The following article from Jakob Nielsen discusses past and current studies about the use of screen real estate. He talks about the impact on usability when app elements are hard to see and hard to manipulate.

- Utilize Available Screen Space:
  http://www.useit.com/alertbox/screen-space-use.html

Context-Sensitive Help

Ideally, your UA is embedded directly in the user interface. This makes it easy for the user to get Help without searching for it. If that is not possible, the next best thing is to use context-sensitive Help. This is a link from the trouble-area directly to the appropriate Help topics.

It is a lot harder to find context-sensitive Help in mobile apps than in desktop apps. The minimal screen real estate may preclude having a link icon or text. The link also adds another code element to the pages where it is employed.

A simple example is shown in PhotoPad in Fig. 5.6. A touch and hold on any of the icons in the tool bar at the bottom activates a "Tool Tip" topic in a message window. The displayed topic corresponds to the icon that is touched. This type of Help is wholly embedded in the app.

Fig. 5.6 PhotoPad: example of context-sensitive Help

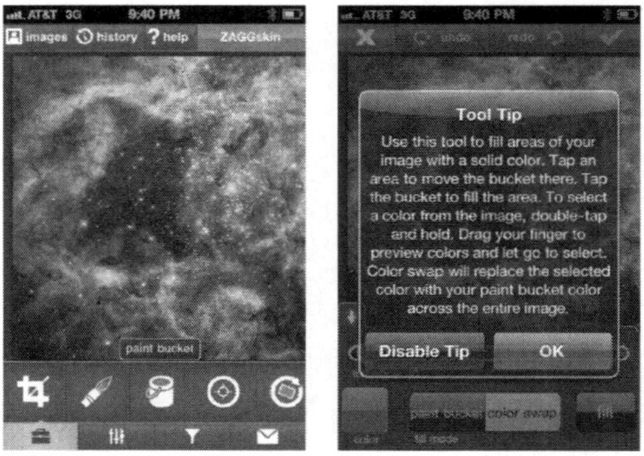

There are many different approaches that a developer can take in creating context-sensitive links. An important factor is whether the content is embedded in the app or downloaded on demand from a server. This subject is discussed in the last section of this chapter, page 68.

Whether you choose embedding or downloading, you will need to get involved with the app development environment. Ideally, you want access to the folder from which the app is calling for your HTML/CSS. That might be located locally or on a remote server.

It also helps to have the current build of the app. This is accomplished with what is called a provisioning file. A provisioning file enables a test version of an app. This set up allows you to post your Help content and then immediately view it on your own mobile device via the provisioned app. Provisioned apps are completely sand-boxed from the versions that are distributed to customers. Your developer will know what to provide you. This is discussed in more detail in the chapters about the individual operating systems.

Help Authoring Tools

For developing browser-based help for mobile apps, you need two tools:

- A text editor
- A browser

Really. It's as simple as that. Mobile Help pages are more about careful design, not volume. Less is more. Pick the right words, thoughtfully lay them out, and layer to other content when needed. If you're working on a Windows system, you can get along just fine with Notepad and IE. On a Mac OS X system, you can use TextEdit and Safari.

Enhancements might include a dedicated HTML/CSS editor. You need an FTP app if you want to post your test files to a server. That's about it. If you find yourself using an automated tool, you may very well be over-designing your UA.

However, if you find yourself with more than a handful of topics and/or you are supporting numerous apps, you may want to look into some tools. The following tools, with the exception of RoboHelp, can be described as "web application frameworks." They manipulate and package standard web files like HTML, CSS, and JavaScript. They each have their own form of authoring. They each create their own unique display of the content.

Dashcode

An interesting tool, included with Apple's Xcode, is called Dashcode. Dashcode is an interactive editor that helps you combine HTML, CSS, and JavaScript to create web applications. You can do a lot of things with Dashcode but one of the pre-designed templates has some interesting possibilities for mobile user assistance.

- Dashcode Browser template: http://www.writersua.com/mobile/dashcode/index.html

The Dashcode documentation describes it best:

> The Browser template creates a web application that supports navigation through multiple levels of content. A web application developed with the Browser template is well-suited to displaying hierarchical information through which users can drill down.
>
> The default web application provided by the Browser template contains a list view for the top level of the content and a detail view for the second level of the content. Selecting an item in the top-level list automatically reveals the detail view associated with that item. You can add additional list levels and you can add content to the detail views.

You can find a detailed tutorial in the Mac OS X developer library:

- Mobile Safari Web Application Tutorial: http://developer.apple.com/library/mac/#documentation/AppleApplications/Conceptual/Dashcode_UserGuide/Contents/Resources/en.lproj/MakingaWebApp/MakingaWebApp.html

Dashcode provides a nice WYSIWYG environment for developing your content, as shown in Fig. 5.7. It also can launch the content in the iPhone simulator (

Fig. 5.8).

It is important to realize that the Dashcode output is all open standard code and can be interpreted by browsers on any platform. If you don't mind authoring on a Mac, Dashcode can be a cheap and easy tool for developing mobile Help files. The output of the Browser template even looks like the solutions we've seen emerging from authoring tool vendors.

Fig. 5.7 The Browser template in the Dashcode editor

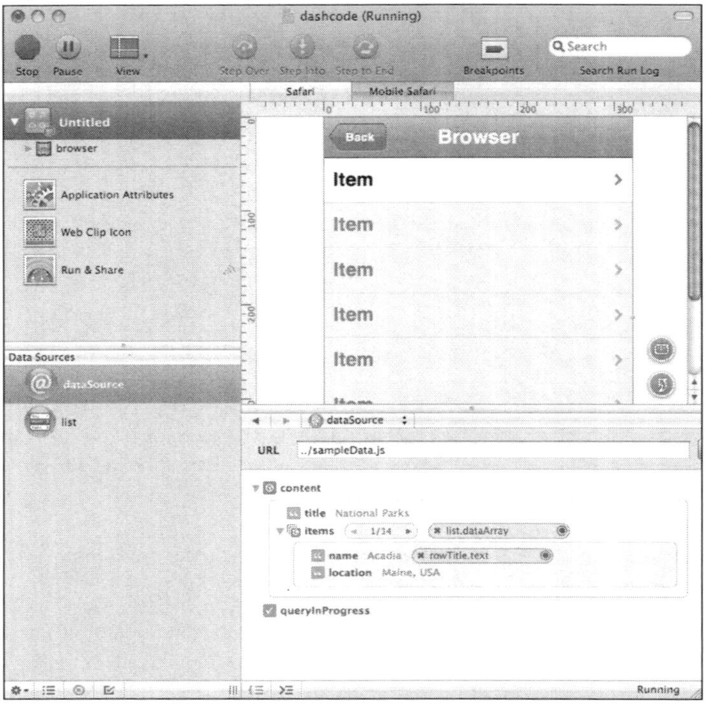

Fig. 5.8 The Browser web app displayed in the iPhone simulator

Flare

The Flare product from MadCap Software has been a popular tool for many years for developing a wide array of desktop Help, including Microsoft Help (HTML Help), web-based Help, and PDF. The product is designed to easily single-source to multiple output targets.

A target they added recently is called WebHelp Mobile. The output is a combination of HMTL, CSS, JavaScript, and user interface images. It is designed to be viewed in a mobile browser as shown in Fig. 5.9.

Fig. 5.9 Flare mobile output

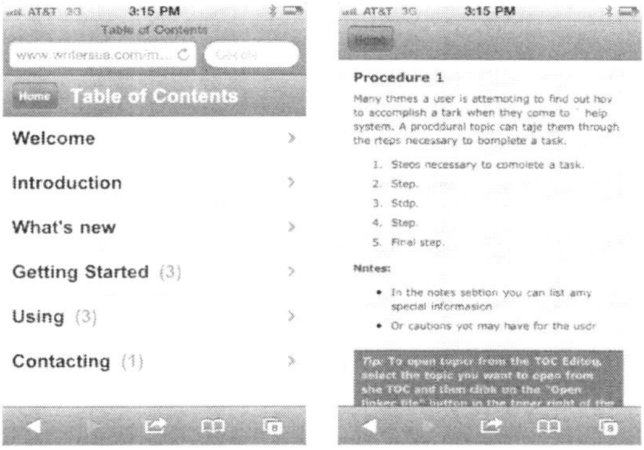

The following page has a sample build of Flare WebHelp Mobile:

- Flare WebHelp Mobile example:
  http://www.writersua.com/mobile/flare/Advanced/Default.htm

Flare provides a simulator for previewing your content, shown in Fig. 5.10a. This saves you the steps of loading your output files onto a server and navigating to them with a mobile browser.

The Flare output can include an Index as shown in Fig. 5.10b. If you have a lot of index entries, it is an unwieldy interface. And if you don't have many index entries you probably don't need an index. The built-in Search (Fig. 5.10c) is a nice bonus feature.

Fig. 5.10 Flare mobile output

a. b. c.

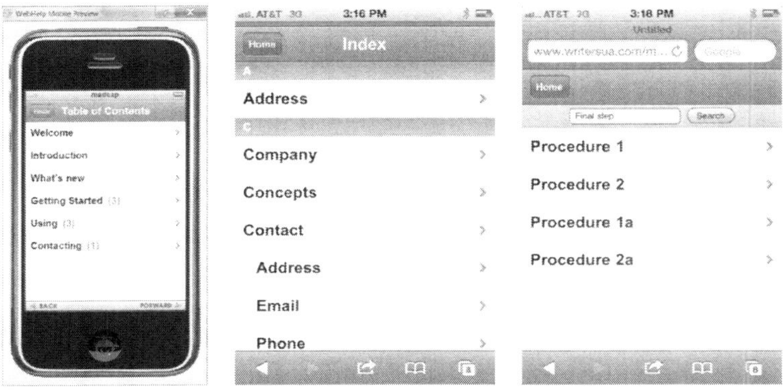

jQuery

An interesting candidate as a home-brew tool for mobile UA is jQuery – the popular free, open-source JavaScript library. The jQuery development team has created a new library that supports touch gestures in a mobile environment. The documentation demo, shown in Fig. 5.11, looks like a really nice hierarchical Help system.

Fig. 5.11 jQuery documentation demo

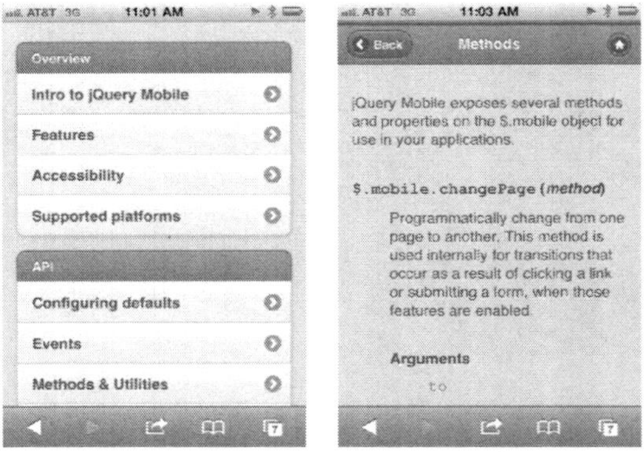

The system consists of a collection of HTML, CSS, and JavaScript. An HTML editor would be your authoring environment. The mobile OS support is pretty extensive considering the newness of this script library.

- jQuery documentation demo:
  http://jquerymobile.com/demos/1.0a4.1/

ePublisher Platform

The ePublisher Platform from Quadralay is a content management system. It provides single-source authoring to a variety of output formats. One of them is to generate a Help system in a web application framework. A unique feature is its ability to recognize the screen size of the device and modify the user interface appropriately.

Fig. 5.12a shows a Help topic displayed in the iPhone. The same topic is shown in displayed in the iPad. With the iPad (Fig. 5.12b), a panel for navigation is added to the left of the topic area. With the iPhone, the navigation page replaces the content being displayed when you click the folder icon.

Fig. 5.12 ePublisher mobile transformation demo

a. iPhone b. iPad

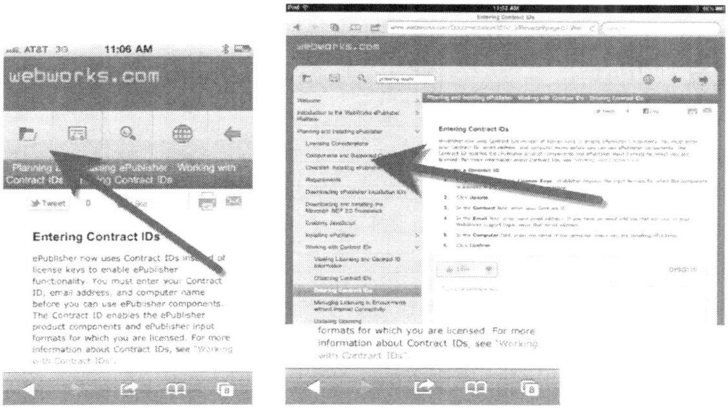

➢ ePublisher sample mobile output:
http://www.webworks.com/Documentation/2010_3/Reverb/#page/01.Welcome%20to%20ePublisher/Planning_and_Installing.5.37.htm

Twister

Backspin Software is in the process of releasing a Help-specific authoring tool in support of mobile apps. Topics can be authored in WYSIWYG mode for iOS, Android, and Windows Phone, as shown in Fig. 5.13. A single source of content can be applied to the different platforms from within Twister. The emulator changes based on the selected platform. The emulator can switch between portrait and landscape mode. There is also a version of Twister that works with Microsoft Word.

The output is in the native mobile app code. This means the look and feel of the Help will match the platform it is running on. The Help files can also be directly linked to the mobile app. For Android and Windows Phone, Twister automatically adds the necessary files and libraries to your project. For iOS, a developer will need to manually make the connection. The Twister libraries include custom buttons that match the style of the apps.

Fig. 5.13 Twister project editor

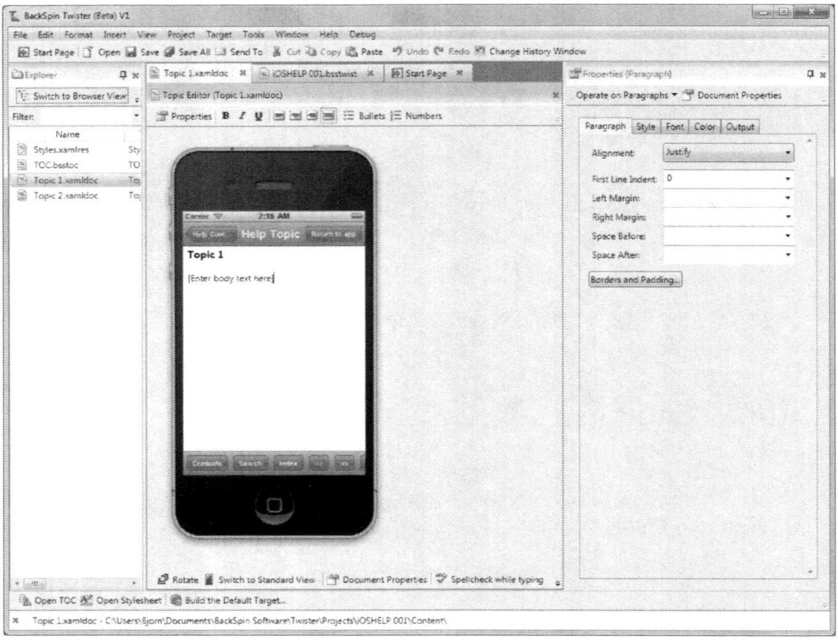

- Twister: http://www.backspinsoftware.com/site/Twister/Twister_Overview.aspx

"Pastrykit"

The Apple iPhone and iPad User Guides are generated with a very complex arrangement of JavaScript, CSS, and HTML. The result is an excellent interface for viewing reference content. The iPad User Guide won the Distinguished Award from the annual competition of the Society for Technical Communication.

The nickname for the technology was "Pastrykit." It was developed as an internal tool with the possibility of providing it to developers. Descriptions can be found in the links below, most dating from 2009.

The technology has since become the basis of the iOS iAd framework. Members of the Apple Developer's Program can get access to the iAd framework. A free tool has been released called iAd Producer. However, the templates in this tool do not seem to be a good fit for user assistance solutions. At this point, this technology is more or less a dead end for UA.

Pastrykit references:

- http://daringfireball.net/2009/12/pastrykit
- http://daringfireball.net/2009/12/more_on_pastrykit
- http://davidbcalhoun.com/2009/pastrykit-digging-into-an-apple-pie

- http://stackoverflow.com/questions/1143589/what-is-the-pastrykit-framework
- http://www.nxfx.com/blog/design-topics/adlib-ipad-javascript-framework/

RoboHelp

The RoboHelp product from Adobe is one of the oldest Help authoring tools. It has provided the ability to create a variety of Help since the early 1990s. RoboHelp supports Microsoft Help (HTML Help), AIR Help, web-based Help, and PDF. An output target they added recently is to the EPUB format. This format is different from the web app frameworks represented by the other tools in this section. EPUB is described in more detail on page 124.

The assumption is that you will have already created your content in RoboHelp for other output targets. RoboHelp uses a conversion script to generate a set of EPUB source files and package those into an EPUB deliverable file. The screens in Fig. 5.14 show a sample Help file as displayed with the Stanza EPUB viewer on an iPhone. The user navigates to topics through the table of contents (a.)

Fig. 5.14 Sample EPUB generated from RoboHelp

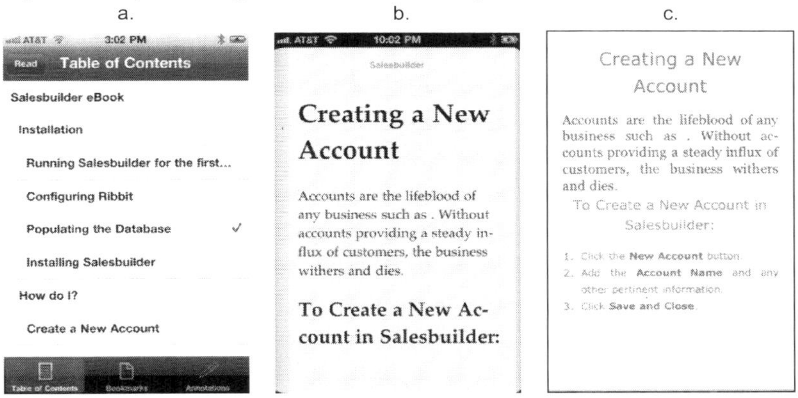

While EPUB is a well-accepted standard for delivering content, it is highly dependent on the users default eReader. You can see the difference in how a topic appears in iBooks (b.) versus in Stanza (c.) Both are popular eReaders, but they interpret the embedded style sheet in different ways.

Testing Tools

This section describes some tools that can be useful in testing your browser-based content.

Testing with Safari User Agents

One of the hidden features of the Safari browser is a "developer mode." You can enable Safari to act like a number of different browsers. The broader term for software that can interpret web pages is "user agent."

If you set Safari to emulate the iPhone or iPad user agents, it will process web content based on the capabilities of those devices. If a site has prepared content for display on a specific device, then it will render that way in your Safari browser.

This feature can be useful in testing a variety of browser-based content – not just mobile. It also works on both the OS X and Windows versions of Safari. Use the following procedure to enable Developer Mode in Safari.

1) Open the **Preferences** box (Edit menu on Windows, Safari menu on Mac).
2) Select the **Advanced** tab.
3) Enable the option to **Show Develop menu**.
4) Close the Advanced dialog box.

   A new option named "**Develop**" appears in the Safari menu bar.
5) From the **Develop** menu, select **User Agent**.

   This opens a list of the browsers that Safari can emulate.

Try testing out the iPhone user agent with sites like ESPN and CNN. Those sites check for user agents and deliver the site appropriately. Fig. 5.15 shows how the Timewerks tutorial looks in the iPhone user agent.

Since there is an ever-increasing set of user agents, it would be nice if you could update the list. And you can. At the bottom of the list is the choice "Other." Click that and you can enter what is called a *user agent string*. Each browser has its own string that describes how it should be interpreted by a server. You'll need to search the browser documentation for the user agent strings you are interested in.

Fig. 5.15 Selecting a user agent in Safari

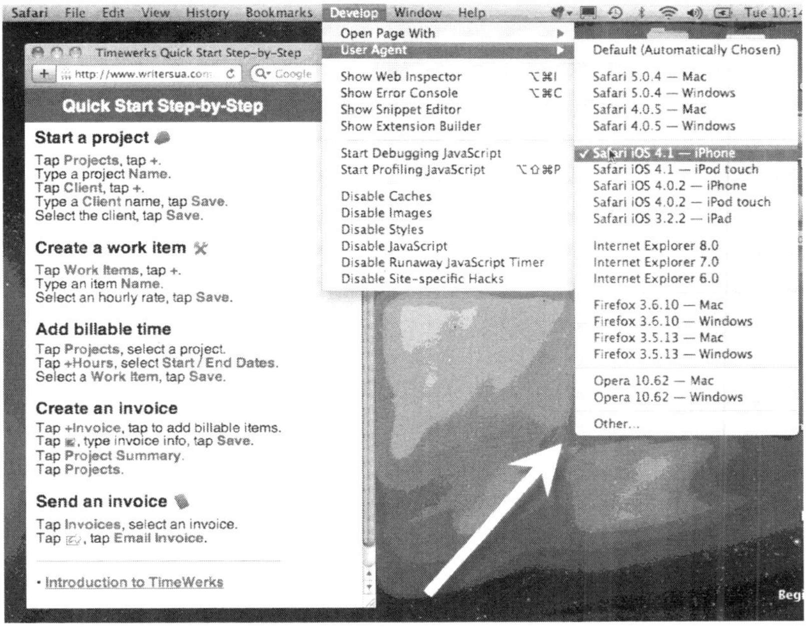

A related tip comes from Lois Karlin. She suggests using the following web site to automatically size the browser window for a device. Lois used the custom setting of 356x500 to approximate the size of an iPhone.

- Set My Browser Size web design site:
  http://setmy.browsersize.com

The following web page provides a list of web sites that have been optimized for the iPhone. These offer some interesting examples of what works and what doesn't when content is customized for a small device.

- Top Sites Optimized for iPhone:
  http://www.iphonelife.com/iphonesites

Testing with simulators

One of the key features of smartphone SDKs is a simulator (called an emulator in Android and WP7). The simulator let you view apps in a desktop environment. Generally, this is only useful if you have access to the source code for your app. However, the simulators offer another useful feature for testing browser-based Help. You can view your content in them.

The browsers in the simulators work just like the browsers in the actual devices. If you load a page in Safari in the iPhone simulator, shown in Fig. 5.16a, you will get a close-to-perfect look at how it will appear when viewed in the actual device. Fig. 5.16b is the Android emulator with an HTC Magic "skin."

You will need to factor out the title and address bars at the top and the tool bar at the bottom of the browser window. These might not be visible depending on how your developers design the link between app and Help.

Similarly, you can test your pages for Android, WP7, and other platforms. Details on the simulators are included in the platform-specific chapters of this book.

Fig. 5.16 Simulators

iPhone Android

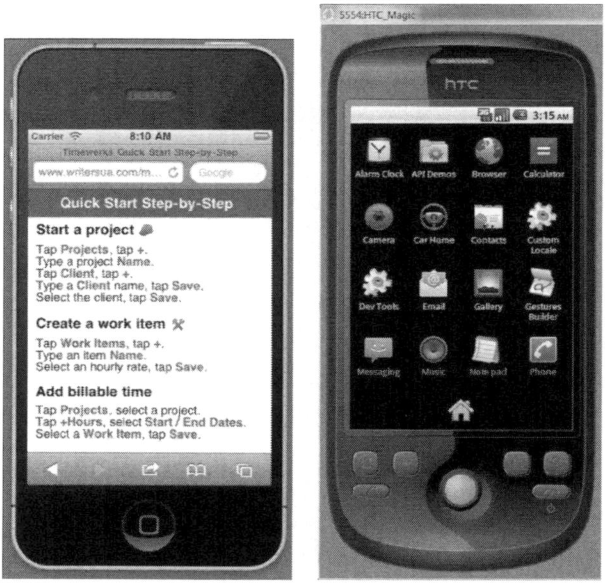

Testing with a provisioned app

If you are working closely with your development team, you can ask them for a special version of the pre-released app. This version is called a provisioning file. The platform-specific sections of this book describe provisioning in more detail. It varies from platform to platform. Provisioned apps are completely sand-boxed from the release versions that are distributed to customers. With a provisioned app, you can test the links from the app to your UA. You can also do usability testing to see if the Help is actually helpful for your users.

How to Deliver Your Help

There are two ways you can deploy browser-based Help. One is by hosting the content on an external server and having the user download it on demand. The other is by embedding the files in the app.

Placing content on a server means that you can update the content at any time. It is also outside of any application approval process (iOS, WP7). However, it won't be available without a connection to the Internet. Since most mobile apps are designed for use with an Internet connection, many app developers go this route. An important downside: there is going to be some delay as the user waits for the content to download. For users on a tiered data plan downloading the Help is going to cost them bits in addition to wait time. Another potential problem is a service disruption, either from your server or elsewhere in the Internet pipeline. Your users will not be able to access Help. This approach is best if you don't want to be part of the app approval process and you have a lot of content.

Embedding your files in the app means that it is always available to be viewed, whether or not there is a connection to the Internet. The downside of embedding is that it makes the UA part of the app approval process. It also becomes part of the application coding time line. Your UA needs to be ready for the various builds of the app. Any changes to the content won't be available to users until the app is updated. This approach is good for essential Help content that has a minimal footprint in terms of file size.

Hosting content on a server

If the web-based Help content resides on a server, there are at least two different ways you might want to organize your workflow. One is for you to hand off your content files to your developers for them to post. The other is for you to do the posting yourself. In either case, you can design and build your Help without the need for a lot of developer support. It will require learning more about your app development environment.

The best scenario is for you to have access to the server from which the app is calling for your HTML and CSS files. Set up one folder for testing and another folder for the final content. This allows you to do all your work in a live setting. You can use the design and testing methods described earlier in this chapter.

When you are ready, you can move your completed Help over to the folder being referenced by the app. Any necessary changes can be posted to the server. If you identify a UA problem after the app is released, you can quickly add new information to the Help folder.

Embedding content in the app

If you are embedding UA content in the app, you will need to work closely with the app developers. There are many ways that the UA can be integrated with the app. The apps shown in Chapter 3, Fig. 3.1 through Fig. 3.6, all have content embedded in the app. You will more than likely be passing off your text and images to a developer to work with. It is a good idea to learn enough about the development process so you can keep up with what is going on. You'll want to know how your information is being called in the app and what resource folders in the source code your files reside in.

6 iPhone and iPod Touch (iOS)

Working within the Apple iOS development environment is pretty pleasant. Apple puts a lot of effort into providing developers with great tools and documentation. It also sets a low bar in terms of the level of hardware/software you need. That's a good thing because you are going to need some equipment and software. You'll also need to learn about how to use the software tools.

Hardware/Software

A common question from newcomers to mobile development is "How can I develop for the iPhone on Windows?" You can't. The development software is designed to be used on Apple equipment and that isn't going to change. You can certainly use VMware or the equivalent on your Windows system. However, you still need to be in Mac OS X when you work with iOS. Fortunately, the basic hardware requirements are very low level. For a computer you need a Mac running Snow Leopard or later. Even older MacBooks that are several years old can run the necessary software just fine.

You need to download the Software Development Kit (SDK). The SDK includes all of the key software for building and maintaining iOS apps. There is a lot more in the SDK than most UA professionals will need. The main item of interest is Interface Builder.

The iOS SDK used to be free but there is now a nominal charge of $4.99 through the Mac App Store. If you haven't already installed the App Store, you'll need to do that first. Then search for *Xcode*.

Purchase and install the app. It is over 4GB in size and will take some time to download.

Finally, you need an iPhone. While the SDK provides a simulator, you really need a phone to effectively test your work. If you are going to be supporting iOS in a professional capacity, having an iPhone is very important.

There is a lot of great information and downloads in the iOS Dev Center. However, you need to be a member and the fee is $100 per year.

- iOS Dev Center (membership req'd): http://developer.apple.com/devcenter/ios/

Knowledge

Once you have your hardware and software you will need to roll up your sleeves and learn how to use what you have. There are three areas that are important to iOS development: Interface Builder, Objective-C, and WebKit/Safari. Only the first is required knowledge for user assistance. The other two will make you a more valued team member.

An excellent book is *Beginning iPhone 4 Development* by Dave Mark, (9781430230243). It is very helpful and well written. It is available in print and EPUB. An especially nice feature is the set of sample files. The sample files are free, whether you buy that book or not. This book will be referring to those sample files.(Thanks to Dave for granting permission to use his examples in this chapter.)

- iOS Source Code Download:
  On the following page, click the Source Code tab.
  http://www.apress.com/9781430230243

Interface Builder

The Interface Builder is called IB for short. IB is an interactive wizard for assembling basic user interface elements. This is the same tool used by thousands of iOS developers. Besides being of use for user assistance, it can provide you with an inside look at how your app is put together.

The area where it helps UA is in developing user interface text. The built-in simulator makes it easy to test your UA directly without the need for help from programmers.

Working with Interface Builder

IB is very easy to use once you know the basics.

- Open the **04-Control Fun** folder from the Beginning iPhone 4 Development sample file download.
- Open **Control Fun.xcodeproj**. This is the project file for this particular demonstration app.

  IB automatically recognizes the xcodeproj extension and opens the project file. What you'll see is the basic IB project window, shown in Fig. 6.1. Controls are in the button bar at the top. Navigation to different sections of the project is on the left. File listings are in the upper right pane. Code will appear bottom right.

Fig. 6.1 Xcode project window

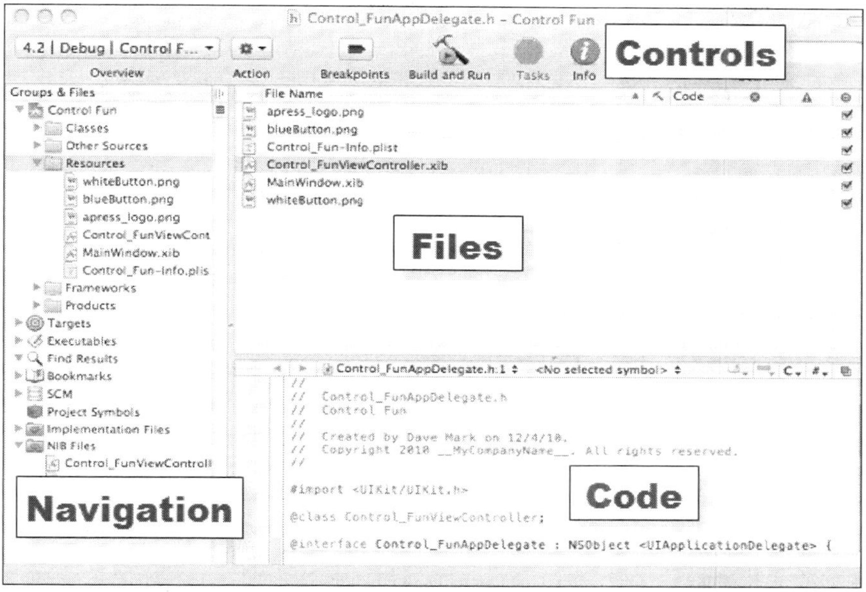

Working with the simulator

Before you do anything else, build and run the project in the simulator.

1) Find the list box in the top left corner of the window. Make sure the current selection is "**Simulator**." See Fig. 6.2.

2) Click the green arrow on the **Build and Run** icon.

Fig. 6.2 Interface Builder Toolbar

The Simulator, Fig. 6.3a, looks like the iPhone and displays the project file home page. You can move the Simulator window by clicking and dragging. The home button on the iPhone image works just like it does on the actual device.

3) Click the **Home** button.

You should see an icon for the Control Fun app. Two of the default apps, Safari and Photos, appear at the bottom of the window.

Fig. 6.3

a. iOS simulator b. Simulator Hardware menu

If you click Safari, it will bring up the mobile browser. Note that it is a live browser. If you are connected to the Internet, you should be able to navigate to a URL.

4) Click the **Home** button and then click the Control Fun icon.

Notice that you can click the buttons and slider, and enter text. With the exception of touch controls, you can really get the full app experience.

You can also simulate different types of hardware and physical manipulation of the hardware using the Hardware menu, shown in Fig. 6.3b.

5) Press **command-Q** to close the simulator.

Working with user interface text

Interface Builder is the place where you can make changes to the user interface text of an application.

1) Return to the Interface Builder project window.

2) Click on the **Resources** folder in the left pane.

Find the **Control_FunViewController.xib**. This is called a "nib" file.

3) Double-click to open it.

The nib file is the gateway to the WYSWYG objects that make up this application.

The window that opens on the right is not one you will work with. You can ignore it but don't close it.

The window that appears on the left (Fig. 6.4) shows the main screen of the app. The contents of the window is referred to as the "canvas." Unlike in the simulator, all the objects on the canvas are selectable. When you click on an object, a shaded border appears around it.

4) Click on the text field that displays "Type in a name"

5) From the Interface Builder menu, click **Tools/Inspector**.

The Attribute box appears for the text field (shown on the right side of Fig. 6.4.) This box contains everything that describes the presentation of the text entry field including the text font, color, size, positioning, and more.

Using the Attributes box, you can experiment with user interface text.

Fig. 6.4 Attributes Inspector in Interface Builder

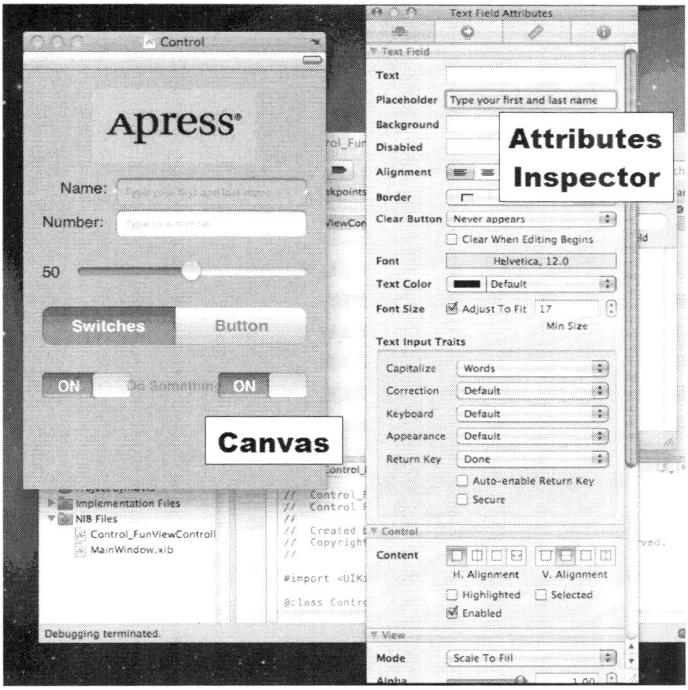

6) In the **Placeholder** field, change the text to "Type your first and last name." Then press Return.

The text in the canvas immediately shows the revised text.

The information in the Attributes Inspector automatically changes as you click on different UI objects.

7) Click on the object that displays "Switches/Button."

This kind of object is called a segmented control. In this type of object, the UI text is in the Title field.

8) Change the text "Switches" to something else and then press Return.

You should see your new text appear on the left hand button in the canvas. Now try adjusting the text in the right-hand button.

9) Click the list box above **Title** and select **Segment 1**.

   Now you can edit that text in the **Title** field.

   So far, you have made changes to the text in two objects. Let's see what it looks like in the simulator.

10) Click on the Xcode window. Then click **Build and Run**.

11) Click the Control Fun icon.

You should see the changes you made in the text entry field and on the segmented control. Congratulations! You just changed the user interface text and successfully displayed it in the simulator. If this were your actual project, you would be able to show this result to usability test subjects and your development colleagues.

Testing with an iOS device

Another way to test your project prototypes is by displaying them on actual iOS devices. Being able to view and work with an app on a device always provides a better review than through the simulator. But there is a catch.

In order to work with devices in this way you need to become an official member of the Apple Developer program. If your team is involved with iOS development already then you will probably be working under that umbrella.

If you are working independently then you need to join the program. There is a yearly fee of $99. You are also asked to submit documentation about your business. This is a convoluted but one-time process. Once you are approved you receive an ID that gives you access to a wealth of developer tools and documentation.

From the Dev Center main page, find the link to the iOS Provisioning Portal.

- iOS Provisioning Portal (membership req'd):
  http://developer.apple.com/devcenter/ios/

The next step is to use the Development Provisioning Assistant. This creates a digital certificate attached to your ID, shown in Fig. 6.5. The certificate is then used to sanction your own devices for use with Xcode. This is called provisioning. You need to provision each device that you want to use for testing.

Fig. 6.5 Provisioning a test device

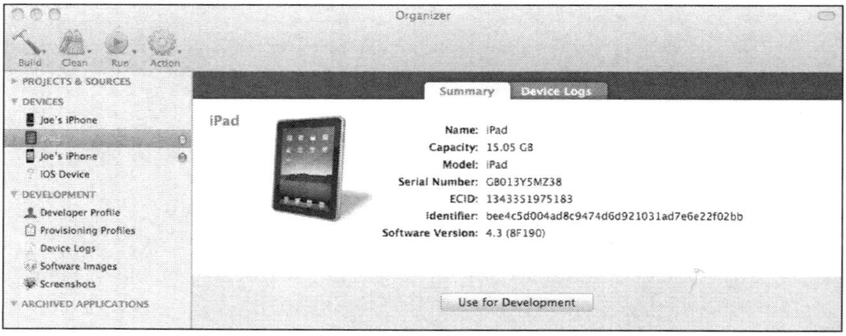

Once that is done, you can start testing your apps.

1) Attach an iPhone or iPad to your Mac.

2) Open an Xcode project.

3) Click the Simulator/Device list box in the top left corner of the project window, as shown in Fig. 6.6.

   Your device name should appear in the list.

4) Change the first pair of options from **Simulator** to **Device**.

Fig. 6.6 Selecting a test device

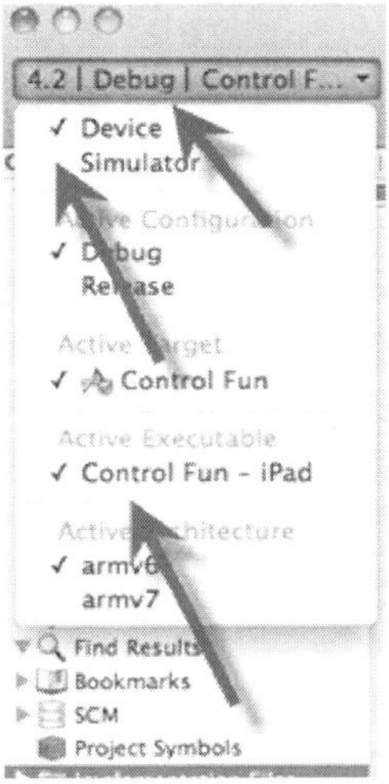

5) Click **Build and Run**.

   Your app should appear on your device as shown in Fig. 6.7.

Fig. 6.7 Viewing a project app through a provisioned iPad

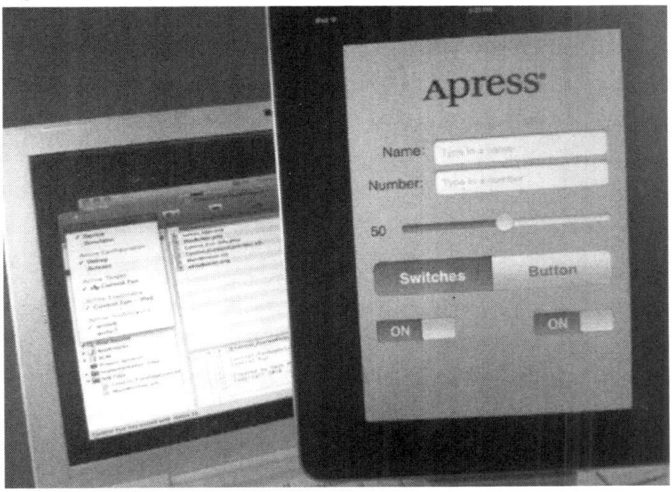

Learning About Objective-C

A lot of UA professionals find it useful to be able to browse through application programming code to find the issues that are relevant to our work. These include calls to context-sensitive Help, UI messages, and resources such as images and logos.

In the Apple world, Objective-C has been a central part of development for Mac OS X and now iOS. Objective-C is an object-oriented variation of the C programming language.

Wikipedia provides a good summary of the technology:

- Objective-C (Wikipedia): http://en.wikipedia.org/wiki/Objective-c

You don't need to be fluent in Objective-C to work with UA but it helps to have a basic understanding of it. Technical writers who specialize in API documentation will probably want to explore it more deeply.

If you already have some knowledge of C then Objective-C will be familiar. There are many books on the subject. Here are a few online tutorials.

- Learning Objective-C: A Primer: http://developer.apple.com/library/mac/#referencelibrary/GettingStarted/Learning_Objective-C_A_Primer/_index.html
- Learn Objective-C: http://mobile.tutsplus.com/tutorials/iphone/learn-objective-c-day-1/
- Learn Objective-C: http://cocoadevcentral.com/d/learn_objectivec/

Learning About WebKit / Safari

WebKit is a technology that renders web pages in browsers. It was originally developed by Apple and then released as an open-source project. From a user assistance perspective the most important thing to know about WebKit is that it is the core component in many of the most advanced browsers. WebKit is the heart of the Safari browser. It has also been adopted for Chrome, WebOS, Kindle, AIR, and many others.

If your users will be viewing any of your UA content on the iPhone or iPad, you will need to know how that content looks and works in Safari. Safari is the center point for the display of all things web in the Apple eco-system. It is on the forefront of standards support and it has aggressively pushed forward with HTML5 and CSS. Safari is also available for other platforms but it only has about 9% share in the overall browser market.

The most important thing here is that Safari on iOS devices is rendered differently than on the desktop. Safari for iOS does not include typical browser controls by default. It is also optimized for the small screen and touch gestures. It is a good idea to review your content in mobile Safari before releasing it to customers.

For more information,

- Official WebKit site:
  http://www.webkit.org/
- WebKit – Wikipedia entry:
  http://en.wikipedia.org/wiki/Webkit
- Safari Web Content Guide:
  http://developer.apple.com/library/safari/#documentation/AppleApplications/Reference/SafariWebContent/Introduction/Introduction.html#//apple_ref/doc/uid/TP40002051
- Getting Started with iOS Web Apps:
  http://developer.apple.com/library/safari/#referencelibrary/GettingStarted/GS_iPhoneWebApp/_index.html#//apple_ref/doc/uid/TP40008134
- Safari HTML Reference:
  http://developer.apple.com/library/safari/#documentation/AppleApplications/Reference/SafariHTMLRef/Introduction.html#//apple_ref/doc/uid/TP40002049

Working with a Project in the Simulator

It can be really useful to work with project builds in the iOS simulator. Your developer can provide you with a build of the app that works with the simulator. It will come as a bundle with a .app extension and the Xcode icon.

1) In iOS 4.3, navigate to:
   <home>/Developer/Platforms/iPhoneSimulator.platform/Developer/SDKs

   Under this folder will be the various platforms supported by the simulator. Find the one you are working with.

2) Click the platform folder name, then click the **Applications** sub-folder.
3) Copy the .app file to the Application folder.
4) Launch the simulator.

   The app should immediately be available in the simulator after you launch it. You can open the simulator without going through Xcode. A shortcut can be found along the same path you just traversed (Fig. 6.8):

   <home>/Developer/Platforms/iPhoneSimulator.platform/Developer/Applications

Fig. 6.8 Location of simulator and simulator apps

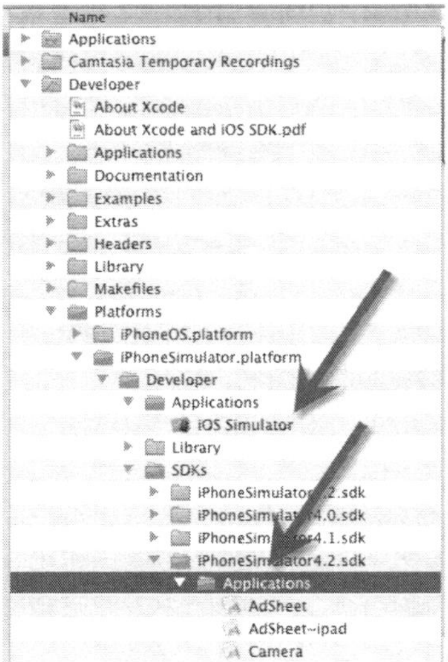

Importing a Provisioned App

If you are working closely with your development team, it really helps if you get your own build of the app to play with. This build is called a provisioned app. It is a fully-functional build of the app that you add into iTunes and sync to update your device.

What you will receive from your developers is a build file and a provisioning file.

1) Connect your device to your computer and start iTunes.

2) Drag the provisioning file into iTunes and sync with your device.

To ensure the provisioned app is installed properly,

3) On your iPhone, tap **Settings**, then **General**.

4) Scroll down to the bottom of the page.

   You should see Profiles with at least one installed, shown in Fig. 6.9. You can click on the profiles to get more information about them.

Fig. 6.9 Provisioning profile

5) Go back to iTunes on the desktop.
6) Click **Library**, then **Apps**.
7) Drag the .app file into the Applications section in iTunes.

   Note: The actual icon for your app might not show up, depending on the stage of development.
8) Sync iTunes with your iPhone as you normally would.

   The provisioned app should now appear on the iPhone.

Screen Captures from an iOS Device

iOS allows you to take screen captures from the device.

1) Hold down the On/Off button.
2) Press and release the Home button.

   The screen image will be added to your Camera Roll in the Photoso app. You can copy images directly from internal storage or sync with iTunes on your Mac.

Screen Captures from OS X

MacBooks have a built-in screen capture utility.

- command-shift-3 for full screen capture
- command-shift-4 for custom size

There are many free and paid-for utilities available with a variety of features.

- Grab utility:
  On your iOA device, navigate to: /Applications/Utilities/Grab.app

- Skitch:
  http://getsatisfaction.com/apple/topics/how_do_i_do_a_screen_capture_on_a_mac

The Safari Debug Console on iOS

Safari offers a debugger for checking browser-based content in iOS devices. This provides a good final check that your HTML and CSS code is set up properly.

1) On your iOS device, navigate to:
   Settings → Safari → Developer (Fig. 6.10a)
2) Set Debug Console to **On**.

   When you display web pages in Safari, a diagnostic panel appears at the top of the window, as shown in Fig. 6.10b.

Fig. 6.10 Setting Debug Console mode on the iPhone

a. b.

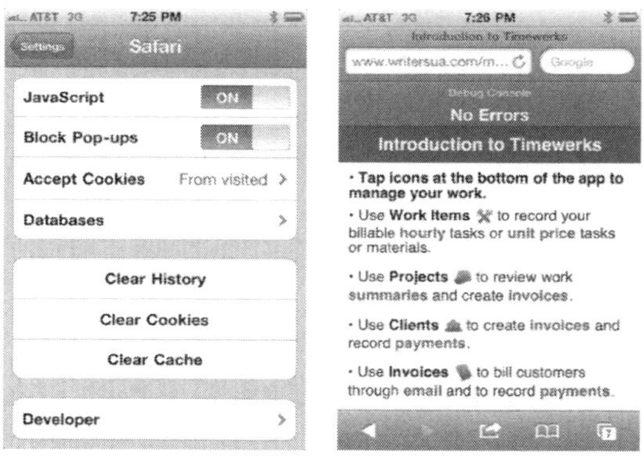

Translation

The iOS platform has a very robust translation / localization scheme. When supporting more than one language, resources for the translated media are stored in separate language bundles. For example, if there is a French and Spanish translation of an app, each of those languages will be represented by a separate folder. The folders contain the translated user interface text, images, sounds, Help files, and any other necessary content.

At the beginning of a project, the development team will choose the default language. The user interface text for the default language will become key values in the translation process. For each language, a strings file is created. This file has the translations for individual words and phrases arranged as pairs as shown in Fig. 6.11.

Fig. 6.11 User interface text – English to German strings file

```
/* Menu item to make the current document plain text */

"Make Plain Text" = "In reinen Text umwandeln";

/* Menu item to make the current document rich text */

"Make Rich Text" = "In formatierten Text umwandeln";
```

The appropriate text is displayed to the user based on the default or self-selected language of their device.

If you are working with user interface text, you will probably just work in the default language. If there are any text changes once translation begins, you will need to update the default and translated text in the strings files.

Similarly, if you are creating embedded Help content, any last minute changes will need to be made to the content in each of the language bundles.

iOS provides many tools to facilitate the process for developers and translators. This information is documented in the iOS Developer Library under "Internationalization and Localization."

Miscellaneous Resources

The following array of resources provides a lot of great information for anyone involved in iOS development.

- Apple Human Interface Guidelines:
  The official Apple publication describing best practices for user interface design.
  http://developer.apple.com/library/ios/#documentation/UserExperience/Conceptual/MobileHIG/Introduction/Introduction.html

- LinkedIn Group – iPhone Developers:
  A networking community specifically targeted at iOS development.
  http://www.linkedin.com/groups?gid=72283&trk=myg_ugrp_ovr

- iPhone Dev Forums
  A collection of resources for iOS developers.
  http://www.iphonedevforums.com/forum/

- "Today in iOS" podcast:
  A semi-weekly audio recording with news and commentary about developments in iOS.
  http://itunes.apple.com/us/podcast/today-in-ios-podcast-the-unofficial/id252820844

- Gallery of iPhone Help:
  Screen captures of Help screens from a variety of iPhone apps.
  http://www.g2meyer.com/gallery/main.php?g2_itemId=5026 Screen captures
- Gallery of iPad Help:
  Screen captures of Help screens from a variety of iPad apps.
  http://www.g2meyer.com/gallery/main.php?g2_itemId=5893

7 Android

Android is a mobile operating system developed by Google. It is unique in that Google is doing the major development and then releasing the code, license-free, to device manufacturers and the general public. Google's aim is to create an ecosystem that drives traffic to its search and other web-based products. While Android started out slow, it has really exploded in the past year. The early 2011 stats include over a 30% US market share for smartphones 300,000 activations per day, and 300,000 apps.

Early versions of the software were buggy and somewhat unattractive. The most recent versions have improved considerably. The device manufacturers are able to customize Android for their own purposes. This is generally a good thing for customers because it provides a lot of choice in the marketplace. However, it is a headache for developers to ensure that their apps will look and operate properly in the many implementations of Android.

Hardware/Software

Android has an SDK like iOS: there is a project editor, a simulator, and the ability to work with UI text and link to web content. Unlike iOS, however, it can be extremely complicated to set up the development environment and difficult to understand how to work with it. If you have experience with Java programming and/or the Eclipse editor, you will definitely have an easier time. You may want to connect with an Android programmer to help you get going. It could mean the difference between spending an hour or a whole day trying to make all the pieces fit together.

A nice feature of Android is that it is platform-neutral. There are distributions for Windows, OS X, and Linux. It is also free. There is no charge for the SDK.

The Android SDK can be very demanding on system memory. You will probably want to have at least 2 GB of RAM on your development computer. The latest versions of Android will need 3 or 4 GB of RAM.

You should get yourself an Android phone. There are so many choices that you should be able to find one relatively cheaply. Get the latest version you can find and afford. Android versions have been progressively more demanding of memory. The latest devices will also support the latest features. You will need to get one that is unlocked if you want to avoid buying a phone contract. You can also unlock it yourself if you have the time and interest in working through the process.

Installing the Android SDK

Whereas Apple provides you the SDK and tools all in one neat package, Android is more like a scavenger hunt. The Android Developer site has good documentation to lead you through the process. There is a great installation guide that has links to all the relevant downloads:

- Installing the SDK:
  http://developer.android.com/sdk/installing.html

It sounds simple but there are many potential pitfalls along the way. Make sure you get the latest versions of the software. Follow the steps carefully and in order.

The following are the broad steps. The detailed steps can be found in the document referenced above.

1) A. Install the Java SDK.

   You might already have this on your system if you work with a lot of software development tools. It is probably a good idea to install it again just to make sure you have the most current version. There are some version dependencies between the JDK and the Android SDK.

1) B. Install the Eclipse editor, shown in Fig. 7.1.

   The Eclipse editor is an open-source tool originally developed by IBM. It provides the same function as Xcode in iOS or Visual Studio in WP7. This is an easy step. Just download and unzip the files. The version was called Helios at the time of this writing. It is constantly evolving.

Fig. 7.1 Eclipse project editor

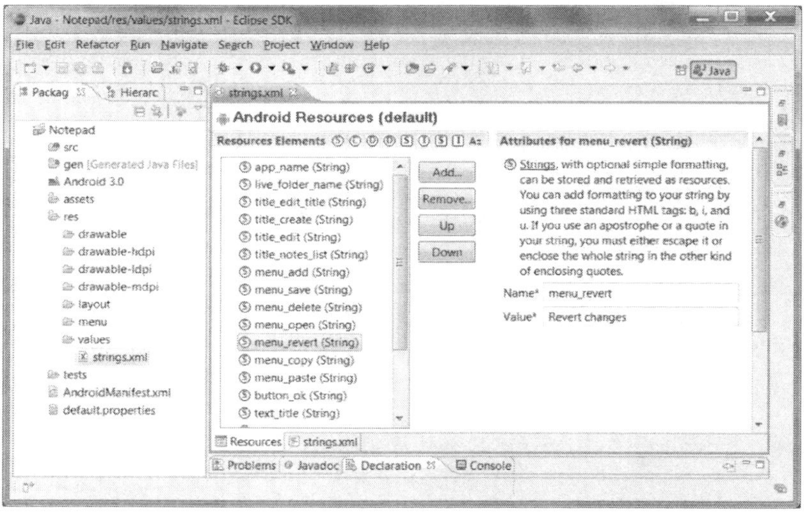

2) Install the Android SDK.

   There are separate versions for Windows, OS X, and Linux. If you are installing the Windows version, you definitely want to download the Installer also. It really speeds things up.

3) Install the Android Development Tools (ADT) Plugin.

   First, you installed Java, which is the foundation framework. The Android SDK you installed lives on top of that. The Eclipse editor provides an environment for working with the SDK. The ADT Plugin provides essential tools for working with specific projects. If you used the Windows Installer, it should perform this step for you. If not, follow the directions in the *Installing the SDK* page.

4) Install platforms and components as described in the *Installing the SDK* page.

   You need to install yet more tools. The Windows Installer doesn't cover this step. Follow the Installation instructions and use Eclipse to download the necessary items. One of the key items is a set of "AVDs." This is described in the next section. The AVDs make it possible to display apps in different versions of Android through the emulator. This step also gives you a taste of working with Eclipse if you haven't done so already.

If you're lucky and/or gifted, your Android system should be ready to work with. There are sample projects included in the SDK. The *Installing the SDK* guide has links to helpful tutorials. You are also ready to bring in your own project files if you have them.

Fine-tuning memory in Windows

The Eclipse editor is very demanding on system RAM. Use the fastest machine you have available. It helps to modify the default settings in Windows for the use of Permanent and Heap memory.

1) In the root folder for your Eclipse files, find **eclipse.ini**. Open it with a text editor.

2) Change the following parameters:

   --launcher.XXMaxPermSize**256** to --launcher.XXMaxPermSize**512**

   -Xmx**384**m to -Xmx**512**m

3) Save and close the file.

   If you are knowledgeable about system memory, you might have your own preferred settings.

Android versions

Support for Android devices is difficult but not rocket science. One of the biggest problems is that there are so many versions of Android and so many devices that have been made for each version. The version issue creates a moving target for developers. The decision on which versions you support will probably not be yours to make. Just know that this might affect how you build and distribute your UA.

At the time of this writing, six major Android versions (Table 5) have been released to device manufacturers and the public. The updates seem to come at a fierce pace from Google. This provides customers with lots of innovation, but it also means there is a fragmented installed base to support.

None of the released versions has been discontinued. All are in use to some degree with mobile devices. The version names are based on sweets. You can find a set of sculptures at the Googleplex in Mountain View representing each version (Fig. 7.2). Froyo (Frozen Yogurt) is the current leader in market share.

You will need to refer to Table 5 as you work with your Android projects.

Table 5 Android versions

v.#	Name	API Level
1.5	Cupcake	3
1.6	Donut	4
2.1	Eclaire	7
2.2	Froyo	8
2.3	Gingerbread	9, 10
3.0	Honeycomb	11
3.1	Honeycomb	12
??	Ice Cream	??

Fig. 7.2 Android sculpture garden

Android Virtual Devices

As developers build and test their apps, they work with what are called Android Virtual Devices (AVDs). AVDs simulate on the desktop how an app will look and work on a device. An AVD is defined by the platform version it supports and the skin it wears. Skins for AVDs are developed by Google, by device manufacturers, and by interested third-party developers. Fig. 7.3a shows a generic skin from Google for the G1 phone. Fig. 7.3b is a skin by a third-party for the HTC Magic.

Fig. 7.3 Android Virtual Devices

a. G1 b. HTC Magic

The AVDs are built with a virtual keyboard displayed in an adjacent space.

To add a new AVD

If your organization is developing an Android app, you should be able to get the AVD definition and skin from your developers. If you are supporting multiple devices, you can use the baseline AVDs provided by Google in the SDK. These AVDs approximate the size and features of an Android device.

Skins for AVDs are available from third parties and can be incorporated into your Eclipse editor. Regardless of where you get your skins, they will consist of a number of files in a folder.

1) If you are using a custom skin, copy its folder to the **skins** folder of the Android version you want it to work with.

   This is where the API level in Table 5 comes into play. The AVDs are referenced by API level number, not by version number. For example, in Fig. 7.4, the files for the G1 skin are in a folder called **HVGA-P-G1**. This folder has been added to the **android-7/skins** folder. Android API Level 7 corresponds to version 2.1 Eclaire.

   You might want to put a copy of all your skins in the platforms folder. Then they are handy when you want to add the AVD to a certain platform version. Or you could add all AVDs to all platforms.

2) From the Eclipse **Windows** menu, select **SDK and AVD Manager**.

   During Step 4 of the initial installation, you installed components using the AVD Manager. You will become familiar with that area. The Manager is where you add new AVDs to your development environment and assign them Android version numbers.

3) Click **Virtual Devices**.

   This displays your list of installed AVDs. You can add new AVDs or edit existing ones.

4) Click **New**, then type a name for the AVD.

   This name is just for your reference so you can recognize the kind of skin and the version it applies to.

5) From the **Target** list, select the version you want this AVD to work with.

   A virtual device must be tied to a specific version of Android. If you want to use a skin with multiple versions, you need to create a virtual device for each.

6) From the **Built-in** box, select your new AVD.

7) Click **Create AVD**, then close the AVD Manager.

Fig. 7.4 The folder for an AVD skin

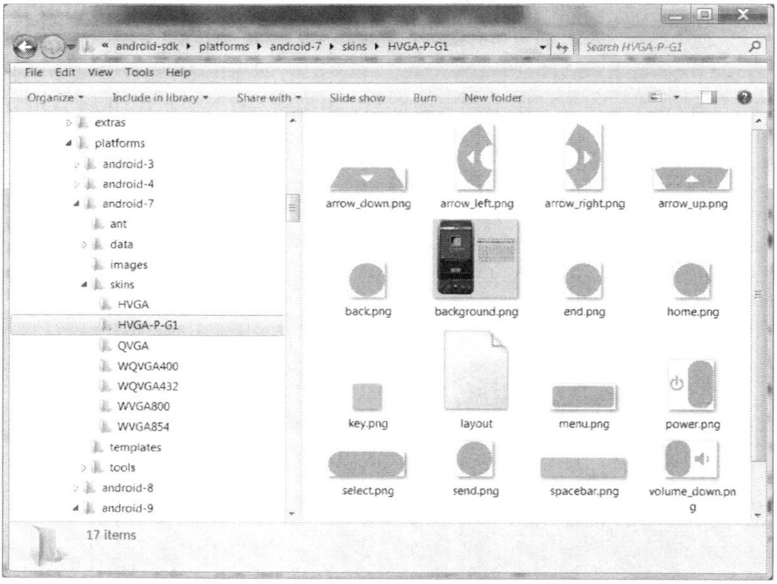

To test an app in the emulator with a new AVD

Now you can use your new AVD with your projects.

1) From the **Run** menu, select **Run Configurations**.
2) Click **Android Application** and then the project you want to work with.
3) Click the **Target** tab.
4) Select the checkbox next to the AVD you want to use.

   Click **Refresh** if you don't see your new AVD in the list.
5) Click **Apply**, then **Run**.

   Your project should appear in the emulator with the selected skin. The newer the API level, the longer it takes to build a project and the more memory the build will require.

To test an app with an Android device

You can run an app on an Android device for testing. This is the best way to review user assistance elements prior to product release. Unfortunately, it is a very convoluted process.

1) Connect your Android device to the computer which has the SDK installed.
2) On your device, enable debugging. Click **Settings → Applications → Development**.
3) Enable **USB debugging** by selecting the checkbox as shown in Fig. 7.5.

Fig. 7.5 Debugging mode on an Android device

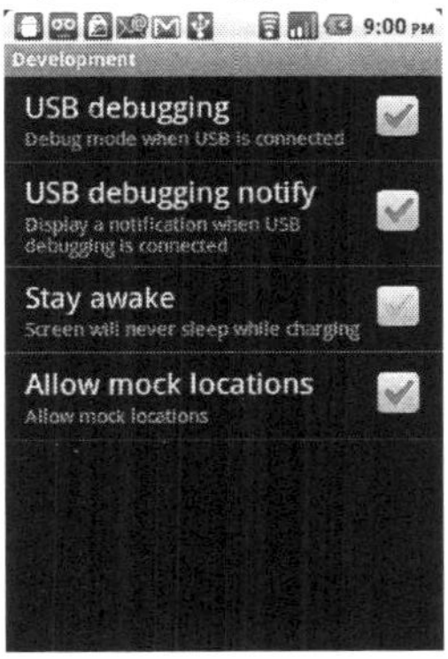

4) In Eclipse, display the subfolders for your project in the **Package Explorer** window.

5) Double-click **AndroidManifest.xml**. This opens the Android Manifest in the center section of the editor.

6) In the Android Manifest window, click the **Application** tab.

7) In the Application Attributes section, find the **Debuggable** list box. It is in the right-hand column of attributes.

8) Select the **true** option. This is a one-time adjustment. You do not need to repeat steps 3-7 again.

9) From the **Run** menu, select **Run Configurations**.

10) Click the **Target** tab.

    This is the same dialog box used in the previous procedure for testing an app with the emulator. In that procedure, you chose the AVD to use with the emulation.

11) Enable the **Manual** setting, as shown in Fig. 7.6.

    The **Deployment Target Selection** mode is your toggle between testing with a device and the emulator. **Manual** is for a device. **Automatic** is for the emulator.

Fig. 7.6 Enable Manual setting for device debugging

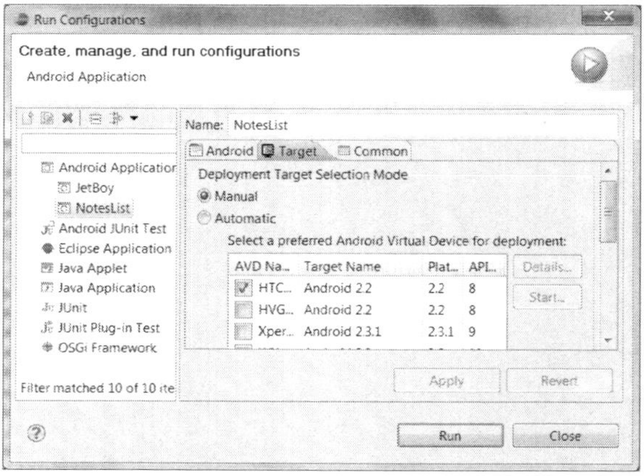

12) Click **Run**. The **Android Device Chooser** window appears.

13) Select your device from the list at the top, as shown in Fig. 7.7.

    You will likely only have one device. But if you have more than one connected to your computer, they will all appear here. Move on to Step 13.

    If you don't see your device, you might need to install a driver. There are separate drivers for every device. Step 3 of the following resource provides details on how to do this.

- Using Hardware Devices:
  This section of the Android Developers Guide describes the device testing process.
  http://developer.android.com/guide/developing/device.html

Fig. 7.7 Android Device Chooser

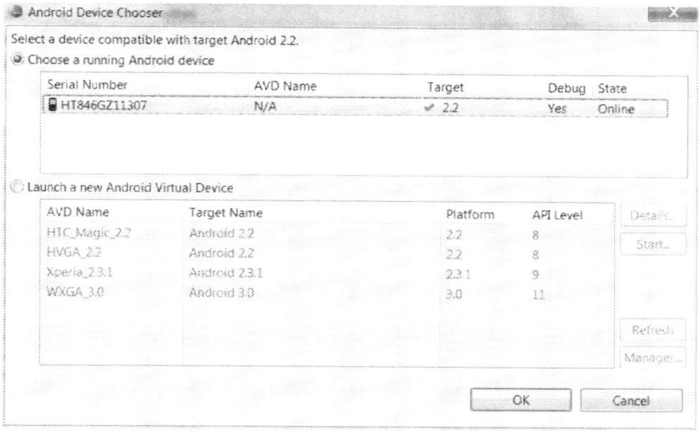

14) Click **OK**. If the OK button is not enabled, make sure you selected your device from the list at the top.

    The app will begin installing on your device. You can view the installation progress messages in the Console tab in the window at the bottom of the editor.

Once your app is visible on the device, you can review it all aspects of it. However, the app is not permanently installed on the device. If you change to another app or the home screen, you will need to click Run again. You do not need to repeat the steps in this procedure.

User Interface Text

Android resources are stored in XML files which include the text strings used for user interface text.

To work with user interface text

1) From **Package Explorer**, select your project.
2) Double-click the **res** folder. This is your Resources folder.
3) Double-click the **values** folder.
4) Double-click **strings.xml**.

    This reveals a list of all the text elements in the project, as shown in Fig. 7.8. They are listed as variable names. To view or edit the text, click on the variable names. The variable name and the associated UI text appear in the right-hand window.

To change the text elements:

5) Type the change in the **Value** field.

6) Click **Run** to build and run your project.

   Eclipse will ask if you want to save your changes if you have not saved them.

Fig. 7.8 UI text editing in Eclipse

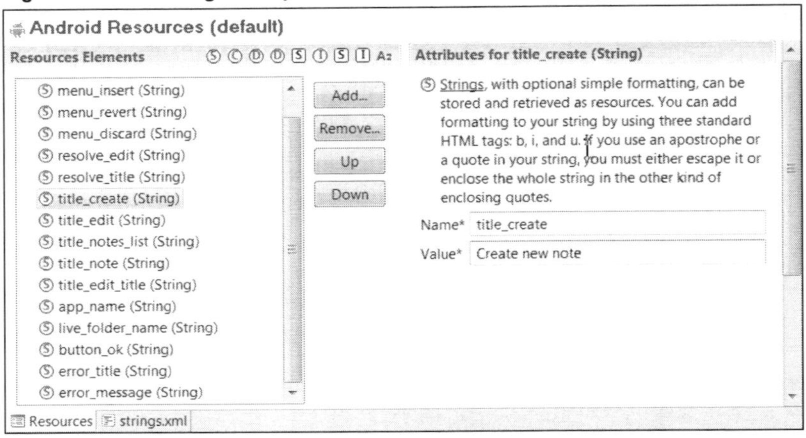

Screen Captures from an Android Device

Capturing images of apps from a device is not as easy in Android as with iOS. In iOS, you can grab any screen at any time by holding down On/Off and pressing Home. No special software is needed.

For Android you need to have the SDK installed. Assuming you do, the capture process is pretty straightforward.

1) Connect your Android device to the computer which has the SDK installed.

2) On your device, enable debugging. Click **Settings → Applications → Development**.

3) Enable **USB debugging** by selecting the check box as shown in Fig. 7.5.

4) Navigate to the main folder for your Android SDK and open the **tools** sub-folder.

5) Click the file **DDMS.BAT**.

   This is a debugging tool called Android Debug Bridge (ADB) that is capable of grabbing screens.

6) One of the items in the top left window should be recognizable as your device, as shown in Fig. 7.9. Select your device.

7) From the **Device** menu, select **Screen Capture**.

   A window should appear showing a rendering of the current screen on your device.

8) To capture the screen, click the **Save** button. Specify a path and file name. The file will be saved with the PNG format.

9) To capture a different screen, navigate to the screen on your device. In DDMS, click **Refresh**. This should reveal the current screen.

   You might want to turn off the Android debug setting when you are done.

   Note: Using DDMS does not require launching the Eclipse editor.

Fig. 7.9 Screen captures using the debugging tool

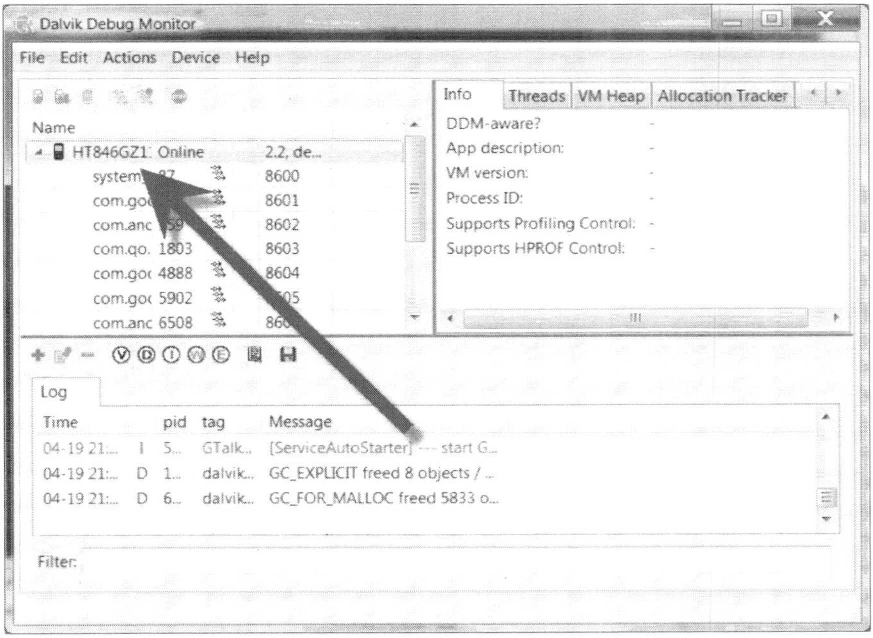

Android-based Tablets

For information about tablets, see *Working with Android-based Tablets*, page 117.

8 Windows Phone

Windows Phone 7 (WP7) is a mobile operating system developed by Microsoft. Unlike Apple, Microsoft is only involved with the OS, not the hardware. However, they have a number of technical requirements that manufacturers must adhere to if they want to use the WP7 software. Unlike Google, Microsoft is not creating their operating system for free. They charge manufacturers to install WP7 on their devices.

WP7 is a dramatically different system from previous versions of mobile software developed by Microsoft. The new design reflects a new way of thinking about how people may want to interact with their devices. The platform line is off to a bit of a shaky start in terms of sales. The partnership between Microsoft and Nokia and the purchase of Skype should result in more positive results in the coming year.

Hardware/Software

WP7 has an SDK like the iPhone: there is a project editor, a simulator, and the ability to work with UI text and link to web content. Like the iPhone, but unlike Android, it is very easy to work with the development tools.

Developing for WP7 requires Windows 7 and various other software applications. There is no charge for the SDK. The WP7 SDK does not require any special hardware configuration. Experience with C# programming and/or the Visual Studio editor is helpful but not necessary.

You should get yourself a Windows Phone. Some of the models have been less successful than others and therefore can be purchased more cheaply. There have not been any significant updates to WP7 as of mid-year 2011. Any phone you get should be as capable as any other. You will need to get one that is unlocked if you want to avoid buying a phone contract. You can also unlock it yourself if you have the time and interest in working through the process.

Installing the WP7 SDK

The WP7 SDK is free for developers. The installation requires Windows 7, Zune, a Microsoft Live account, and many software applications. The software downloads are extensive and bulky. However, the install process is fully automated. While WP7 installation is more difficult than iOS, it is much simpler than Android.

Follow the directions at the sites listed below. You must use Internet Explorer when working with Microsoft web sites. The sites seem to be optimized for IE, and other browsers will often not render the pages correctly.

- Getting Started Guide:
  http://create.msdn.com/en-us/home/getting_started

To set up your development environment

The installation software takes care of getting everything installed properly on your system. If you are not familiar with Visual Studio, this section will get you started.

1) Launch **Visual Studio 2010 Express for Windows Phone**.

2) Click **New Project** and then select the **Windows Phone Application** from the list of sample apps. That is a good demo to start with.

   The editor opens with multiple windows representing different part of the sample project, as shown in Fig. 8.1. You may want to close several windows: Document Outline, Error List, Solution Explorer, and Class List.

   What is left are the MainPage window on the left and the Properties window on the right. The MainPage window features a WYSIWYG view of the main app screen appears. This is referred to as the "canvas."

3) Click the **Zoom to Fit** button. Find it on the bottom of the slider shown in Fig. 8.2a.

   The button automatically sizes the canvas. The slider lets you set exactly what size you prefer.

Fig. 8.1 Windows Phone 7 editor

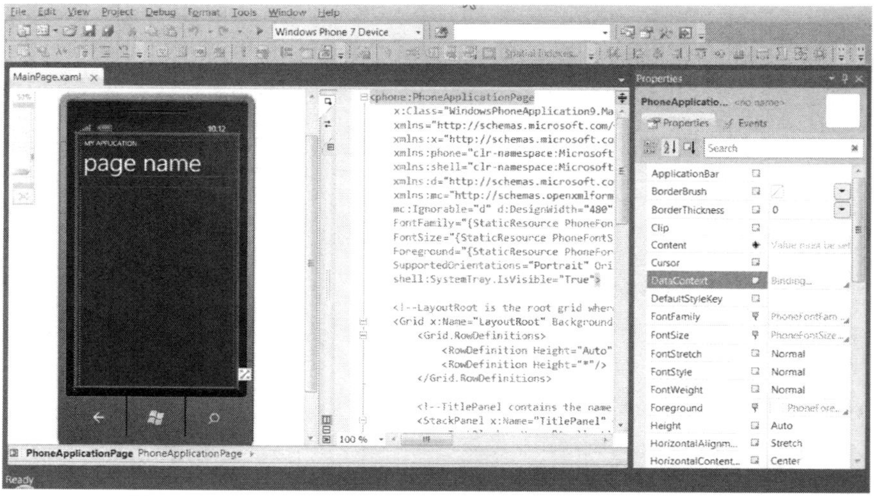

Fig. 8.2

a. Zoom slider b. Target list box

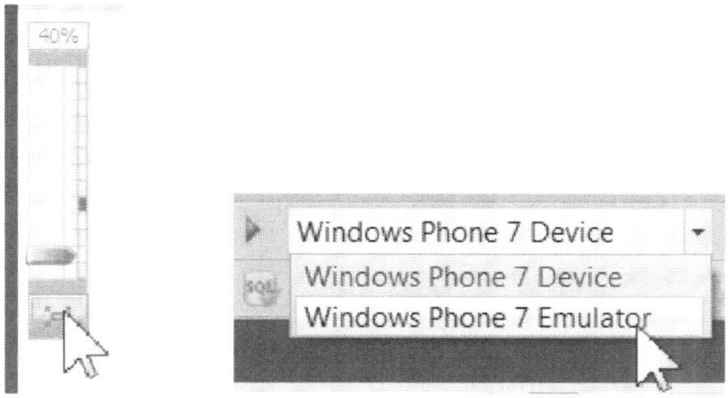

To view an app in the emulator

WP7 provides an emulator for working with smartphone apps. This procedure corresponds with the sample file described in the previous section.

1) In the Standard toolbar, click on the target list and select **Windows Phone 7 Emulator**, as shown in Fig. 8.2b.

   You don't need to build the solution. Just run the emulator.

2) Click the **Start Debugging** button (the green right-facing arrowhead).

   The default emulator appears as shown in Fig. 8.3a. It is a separate window and can be moved around as needed.

   The emulator has a floating tool bar next to it. The two lowest controls let you adjust the size of the emulator. The middle two controls change orientation between portrait and landscape.

Fig. 8.3 Emulator

a. Default b. HTC Mozart

The home page of the emulator will show the icons for Internet Explorer and Settings. The title of your sample app should also be visible. The IE app is a live window to the web. You can use it to view your browser-based Help if it is located on an external server. Click and hold on the frame of the emulator to move the window.

To add a new skin

As with Android, individuals and organizations are creating "skins" to represent different devices in the emulator. Fig. 8.3b shows the skin for the HTC Mozart phone.

You can find skins on the web. One good resource is:

- XDA Developers:
  http://forum.xda-developers.com

You can also search the web with a keyword phrase like "windows phone emulator skins."

1) Navigate to **Program Files → Microsoft SDKs → v7.0 → Emulation**.

   This section controls the phone canvas within Visual Studio.

   There are four files that make up the default skin: an XML file and three images. The XML file defines the presentation attributes of the skin. The images define how the skin looks. Some skins include an XML file; others just provide the three images. If an XML file is not provided you should use the default XML file.

2) Copy the files for the new skin to the emulation folder.

3) Navigate to **Program Files → Microsoft XDE → 1.0**.

   This section controls the emulator.

4) Copy the files for the new skin to the 1.0 folder, shown in Fig. 8.4.

   The WP7 emulator only supports one skin at a time. You may want to copy the existing files into a backup folder. If you have multiple skins you will need to manage the folders and files manually.

Fig. 8.4 Skin files in the emulator

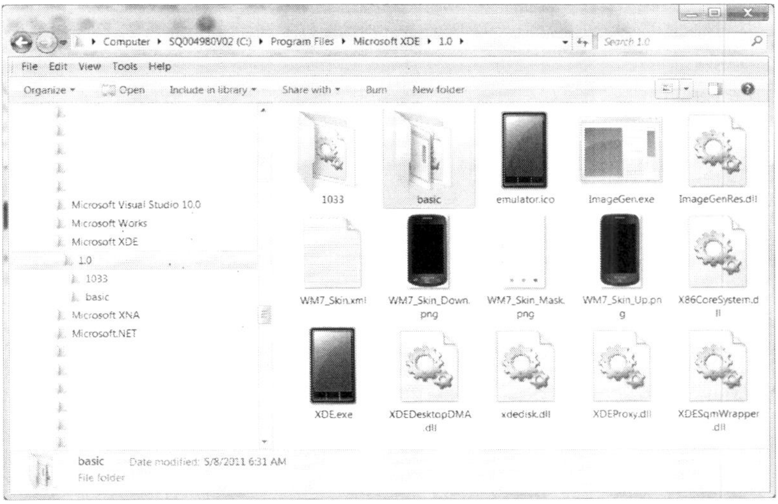

There is no current documentation for skins on the Microsoft Windows Phone 7 site. However, there is content on MSDN for Windows CE that appears relevant. The XML Schema closely matches what is described above. The following article introduces the format:

- Emulator Skin Files:
  http://msdn.microsoft.com/en-us/library/ms905128.aspx

The Emulator Skin XML Schema page provides definitions for the image elements and others. The definitions appear to roughly correspond to the WP7 format.

- Emulator Skin XML Schema:
  http://msdn.microsoft.com/en-us/library/ms905130.aspx

> The normalImage="up.bmp" element specifies the normal art file for the Emulator skin. The normal art file is required for the Emulator skin. The normal art file specifies the size of the window for the Emulator and the appearance of the Emulator skin.
>
> The mappingImage="map.bmp" element specifies the mapping file for the Emulator skin. The mapping file is an optional file that defines the regions occupied by the buttons in the Emulator skin.
>
> The downImage="down.bmp" element specifies the down art file for the Emulator skin. The down art file is an optional file that specifies the appearance of the buttons on the Emulator skin when the buttons are pressed. For more information about art and mapping files, see Emulator Skin Files.
>
> The toolTip="This is my ToolTip." element is an optional element whose text displays when you move the pointer over the button.

Testing with a Windows Phone

Another way to test your project prototypes is by displaying them on actual Windows Phone devices. Being able to view and work with an app on a device always provides a better review than through the simulator. But there is a catch.

In order to work with devices in this way you need to become a member of Microsoft's "App Hub." If your team is involved with Windows Phone or XBox 360 development then you will probably be working under that umbrella.

If you are working independently then you need to join the program. There is a yearly fee of $99. You are also required to submit documentation about your business. This is a convoluted but one-time process. An added benefit is getting access to a wealth of developer tools and documentation.

You need to fill out a profile, set up a login, and pay the fee by credit card. Then you will be asked to send identifying information about your company to Geotrust.

The place to start is on the MSDN App Hub.

- App Hub Registration Walkthrough: http://create.msdn.com/en-US/home/about/developer_registration_walkthrough

Once Geotrust vets your identity, you can register one or more devices to your account. You will not need to go through this part of the process again.

- In the **App Hub**, click **My Dashboard**, then **Windows Phone**.

If the first two items in the checklist are confirmed and validated, you can "unlock" your phone for development. Keep a bookmark to this page. Note: unlocking your phone has a different connotation here than it is does for mobile devices in general. You aren't opening your device up to work with multiple phone service providers. You are just making it possible to link the phone to Visual Studio.

The procedure on the following site guides you through the connection between phone and software.

- How to use the Developer Registration Tool: http://msdn.microsoft.com/en-us/library/ff769508(v=vs.92).aspx

Note: You may need to search around your file system to find the Windows Phone Developer Tools folder mentioned in the procedure. Also, make sure you have named your device in Zune: (phone → settings → name your phone).

Once the above procedure is complete, return to your Windows Phone page in the App Hub.

- In the **Unlock your phone** part of the checklist, click **Manage your development phones**.

You should find your phone listed under Registered Devices. You do not need to do this part of the process again unless you want to register another device. You can register up to three devices.

Finally, you can start testing with your phone.

1) Start **Zune**. You always need Zune running when you want to work with your phone.
2) Start **Visual Studio Express for Windows Phone**.
3) On the Standard toolbar, click on the Target list box and select **Windows Phone 7 Device**, as shown in Fig. 8.5.

Fig. 8.5 Target list box

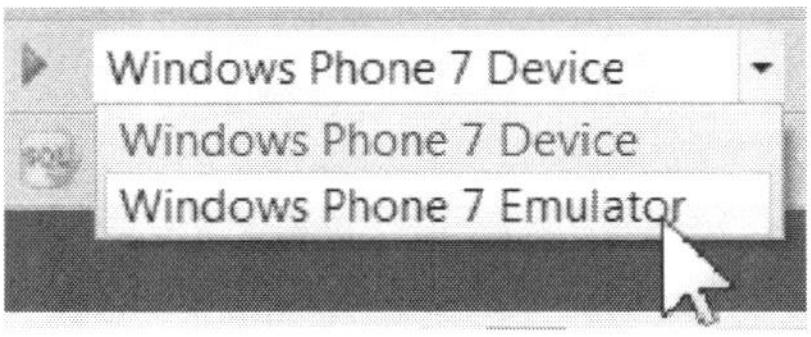

4) Click the **Start Debugging** button (the green right-facing arrowhead).

The screen on the phone will go dark and then your app should appear, as shown in Fig. 8.6. The color scheme of the app in the emulator may differ from how it looks on the phone. The phone is processing the UI based on the Theme settings of the device.

Do not disconnect the phone from your computer while testing. This will sever the connection and the app will disappear from the phone. You can't work with the test app on the phone without the connection to your computer.

Fig. 8.6 Testing an app in a phone

WP7 versions

Windows Phone 7 is completely new and is only loosely related to Windows "Mobile." There was no update path for Windows Mobile users to move to WP7. If you were supporting a Windows Mobile app, you aren't going to be able to carry over much of anything to WP7. If your organization is beginning mobile development with WP7, you don't need to worry about supporting Windows Mobile.

As of this writing, Microsoft has released the first update to WP7, called "Nodo." Microsoft has allowed the mobile carriers to take charge of releasing updates to their customers. This has led to extremely long delays waiting for the updates. Table 6 summarizes the updates announced as of mid-2011.

Table 6 Windows Phone versions

Release	Features
Nodo **(in progress)**	Copy and paste Faster loading of apps Improvements to wi-fi, Facebook, Outlook, and messaging
Mango v7.1 **(Dec. 2011?)**	Improvements to the Marketplace Multitasking Open APIs A gyroscope IE9
Apollo **(Q2 2012?)**	Common apps for Windows 8 and Windows Phone 8 Built-in PDF reader

User Interface Text

Working with user interface text in WP7 is straightforward. You work with the canvas, its elements, and their associated properties. This example is based on the sample application **Windows Phone Application**.

1) Click on the text element "page name" in the canvas.

   The information in the Property window changes (see Fig. 8.7). At the top of the Properties window is the type of element you clicked on (TextBlock). Next to that is the unique name of that element (PageTitle).

2) Scroll down through the properties.

   They are listed in alphabetical order. These properties affect the appearance of the element including UI text, font, and margins.

The Text property controls the UI text. In this example, the text used is "page name".

3) Try typing an alternate name, then press Enter.

   The new text appears in the canvas.

Fig. 8.7 Changing user interface text

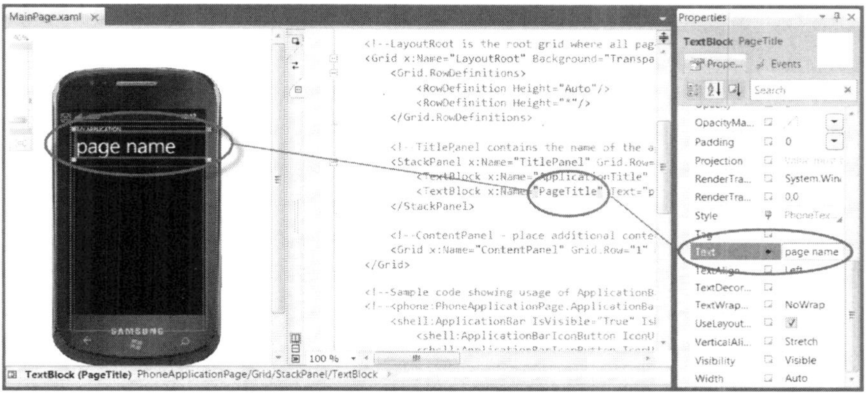

Screen Captures

Unlike with iOS and Android, there is no built-in screen capture facility. You need to use the emulator to load an app. Then use a third-party screen capture utility to grab the emulated image. Of course, this will only work for apps where you have the source code. There is no way to capture screens from the device.

- Comment on screen captures by Microsoft: http://www.anythingbutipod.com/forum/showthread.php?t=60640

9 The iPad and Tablets

The term "mobile" can apply to many different computing devices. Phones are definitely designed to be mobile. So are laptops and netbooks. You can easily pick them up, pack them up, and use them on the go.

The iPad has expanded the definition of mobile to include something bigger than a smartphone and smaller than a laptop. But also, different than a netbook. The important distinction with the iPad was to marry the device size with an "always on," speedy OS, reliance on gestures for input, and an app store ecosystem.

The iPad has definitely defined what success can mean for a tablet. Microsoft first started hawking tablets in 2001 to no avail. The iPad offers a simplicity and comfort that attracts customers. Compared to an iPad, Windows 7 on a netbook does not feel "mobiley" enough.

Fig. 9.1 Tablets

a. iPad b. Galaxy c. Xoom

All of this is not to say that the iPad will be without competition. New entrants to the category are starting arrive in waves. So far, the OS of choice has been Android. The latest version of Android, named Honeycomb, has been designed by Google specifically for tablets. Currently it is only being made available to device manufacturers but that will change soon.

Beyond media hype, the popularity of a product is what drives development of apps for the product. The iPad has already achieved enough traction to make it a slam-dunk choice for most developers. Android and RIM are in the early stages of building out a a substantial catalog of apps. Microsoft appears to be in a holding pattern with no tablets in sight.

The underlying codebase of the iPad more or less ensures starting with a smartphone design and making it bigger. The iOS eco-system of tools, templates, and existing code is based on the iPhone.

On Android, the tablet OS is just another step (3.0) in the evolution of the overall platform. The same development tools used for Android phones are being used for Android tablets. Announcements from Google indicate that this integration will continue to tighten up.

RIM's Blackberry Playbook is based on their own OS called QNX. HP/Palm will be releasing tablets using their webOS. In both cases, these are the same operating systems used for their smartphones.

What this means for user assistance professionals is that working with tablets is going to be more like working with smartphones than working with desktop applications. For iOS and Android, all of the information presented earlier in this book is going to be relevant to tablet design and implementation.

It is not clear what Microsoft's strategy is going to be yet. Will they approach tablets as an expansion of Windows *Phone* 7 or a diminution of Windows 7 as they did with netbooks?

This rest of this chapter will highlight some of the significant differences between tablets and smartphones.

Designing UA for Tablets

The size of tablets creates an interesting design question for developers and user assistance professionals. Let's revisit an illustration mentioned in the first chapter. Fig. 1.4 shows the approximate relative sizing of the screens for various devices. The tablet has about one-fifth of the screen real estate of a typical desktop screen, but still much more space than a smartphone.

It is virtually impossible to downscale a desktop app to work in a smartphone view. It is difficult to do it for the seven-inch Android tablets. However, the iPad size, at ten inches, is definitely doable.

Fig. 9.2 Comparison of screen sizes (values are vertical heights)

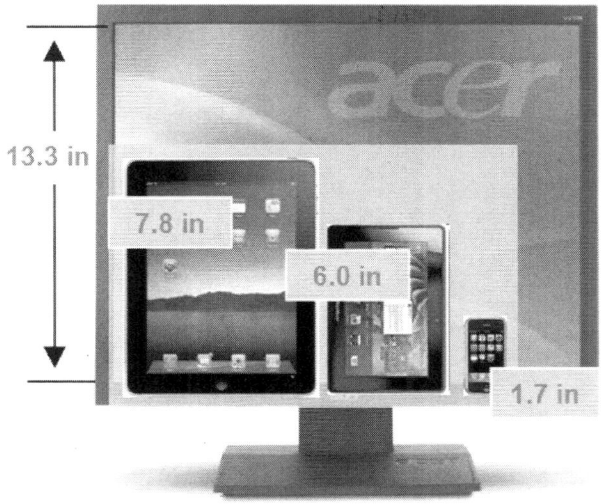

The amount of screen real estate will clearly have an effect on what we can do. There is more room for the apps to stretch out. There is sufficient size to have a reasonably-sized information window. Let's look at how this manifests itself for UA in iPad apps.

The apps in Fig. 9.3 show examples of UA in a dedicated Help section. Both apps use the iOS popover UI element to host the content. This feature is only available in iPad development. Both apps also use a **?** icon to launch the Help.

Despite those similarities, the apps offer up very different presentations of Help content. Touchup (Fig. 9.3a) uses a formal menu structure with links to a series of narrated video simulations. Photocard (Fig. 9.3b) has a more stylized page to guide users into the Help topics.

Fig. 9.3 Apps with a formal Help structure.

a. Touchup b. PhotoCard

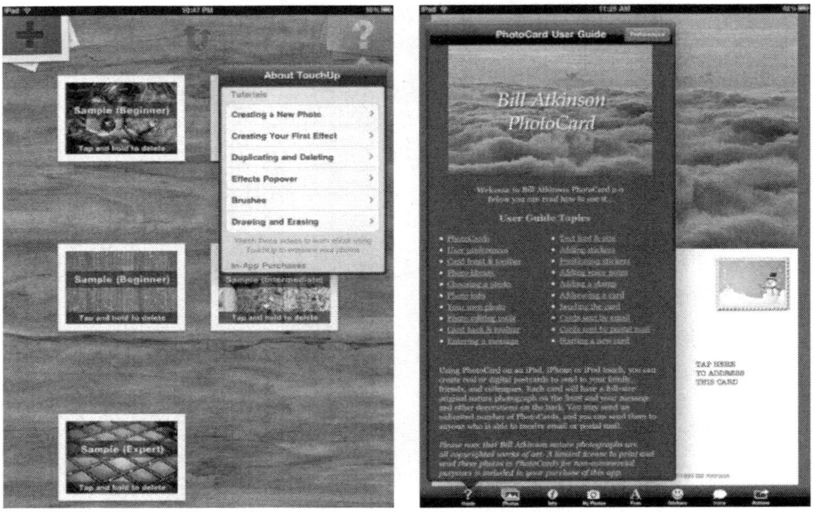

The iPad has enough screen real estate to encourage more visually interesting approaches to UA. Also, the framework of iOS makes it possible to display information in ways that were not practical with desktop apps.

Pulse, shown in Fig. 9.4a, is a threaded news reader that integrates stories from a variety of publications. When you first start using Pulse, helpful information appears as an overlay on the home page of the app. This makes it easy for the user to understand the information presented in the Help. Similarly, the Infinity Blade game (Fig. 9.4b), displays the Help information directly in the action.

Fig. 9.4 Help used in an overlay

a. Pulse

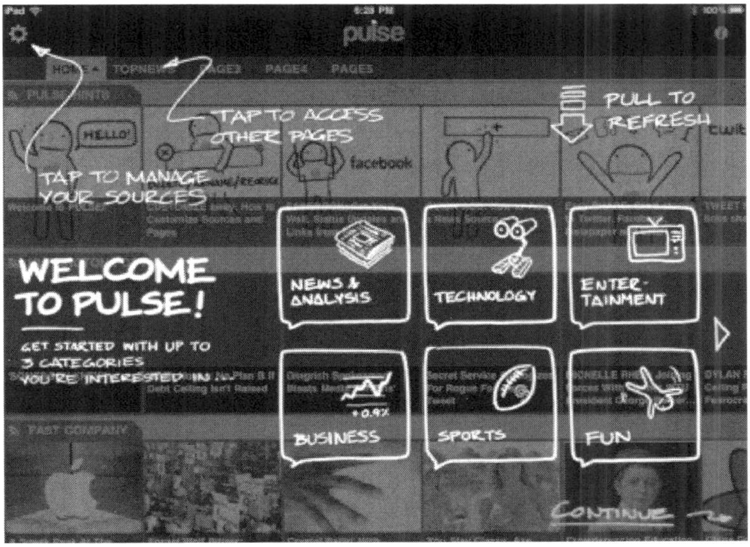

b. Infinity Blade

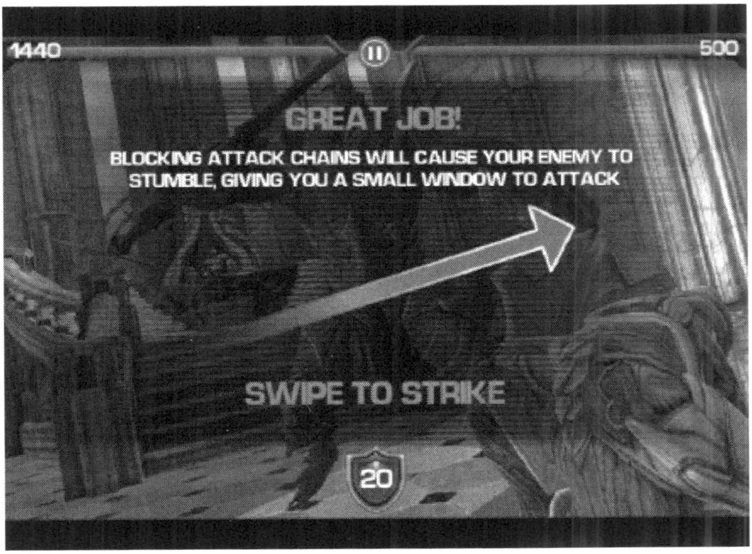

Help information can really resonate with users when it is presented using the features of the app itself. Stickyboard, shown in Fig. 9.5a, lets users create movable note cards. Upon first use, the app displays a page of sticky notes with Help information in them. Popplet (Fig. 9.5b) is a multimedia version of note cards (called popples) where you can have graphics, links, and photos in addition to text. When the user click the Help button at the top, the page fills with Help popples.

While this form of UA may not be possible for most apps, we should always keep an eye out for ways to use the native features of our apps.

Fig. 9.5 Using app capabilities to display UA

a. Stickyboard b. Popplet

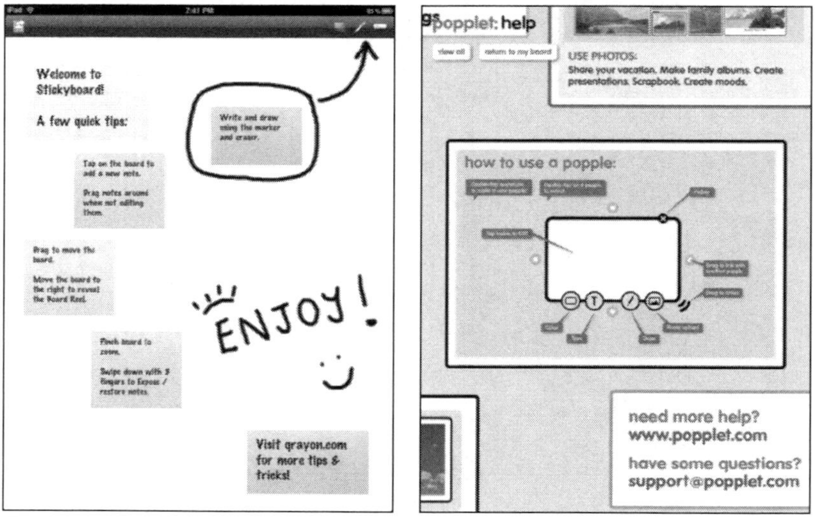

One of the exciting attributes of many popular iPad apps is attention to an attractive visual style. Graphical elements are relied on heavily to frame and enhance the features of an app. User assistance should be considered in that light as well. The MicroStrategy app, shown in Fig. 9.6a, uses inset screen captures to highlight important controls. Sketchbook (Fig. 9.6b) has detailed graphics depicting the multi-touch gestures that activate different features.

Fig. 9.6 Using a graphical style for UA

a. MicroStrategy

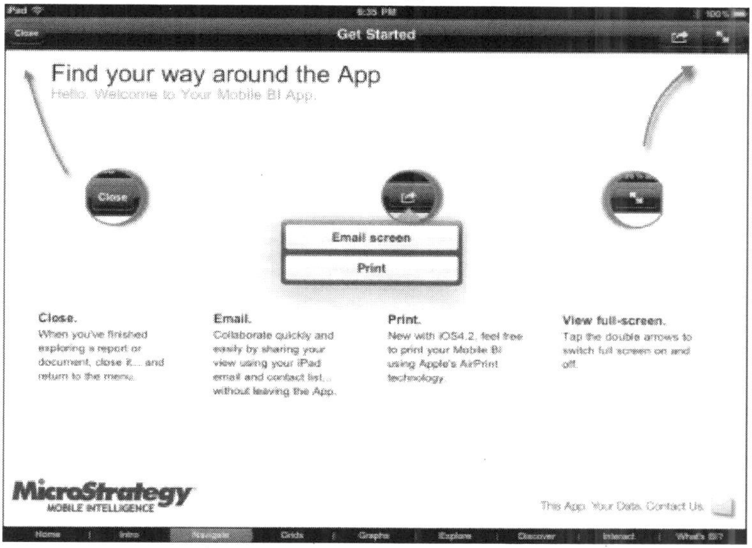

b. Sketchbook

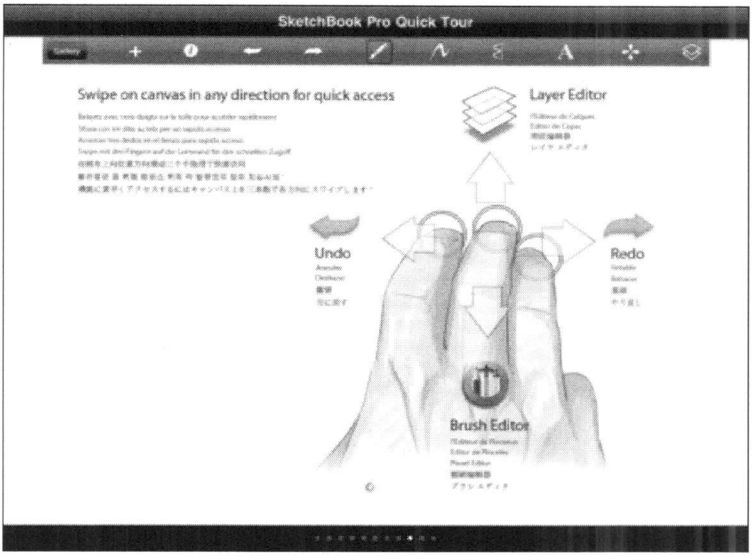

Good user assistance provides a comprehensive array of support choice. As with any type of software, users will benefit from having several options for finding help. In Fig. 9.7a, Pulse offers links to social media sites, a support forum, email, and tutorials. This is in addition to the Help layer described above.

Product web sites are always a good repository for supplemental information. The content can be viewed on a mobile device or through a desktop browser. Popplet (Fig.

9.7b) provides a link from the app to a support web page with frequently asked questions.

Fig. 9.7 Supplementary support

a. Pulse

b. Popplet

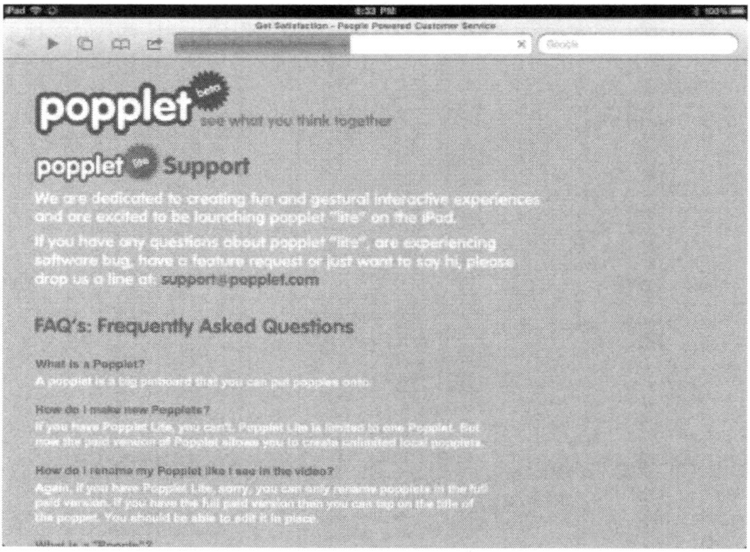

Other design issues

The previous section of the book discussed screen real estate, native capabilities, graphics, and supplemental UA. There are a few other issues to consider.

One of those is the availability of an Internet connection. With smartphones, it is generally assumed that the user will be connected most of the time by cellular or wi-fi. You can more or less count on server-based Help content always being available. It is not as clear with tablets.

While tablets are definitely designed to be connected on a regular basis, many users work with their apps in an offline mode. Approximately two-thirds of iPads are 3G models. The other third likely have wi-fi at home, but outside of that their connectivity is a big question mark. What this means for UA is the need to give careful consideration as to the tradeoffs between server-based and embedded content. This issue was discussed in *How to Deliver Your Help*, page 68.

Speaking of embedded content, the amount of space available to UA is always an issue. The amount of storage in a tablet may not necessarily be any more than in a smartphones. The amount of storage is based on chip capacity and not directly related to the size of the device. While tablets may afford more opportunities for rich content, you will need to know what your UA footprint can be in terms of file size. This is further complicated because the amount of storage varies from device to device.

A final issue to consider is how UA fits into the value proposition for your app. The average price of iPad apps tends to be much higher than for smartphone apps. Phone apps tend to go for 99 cents. iPad apps for $4.95. More robust iPad apps can be ten dollars or more. For consumers, a higher price usually implies a higher level of quality. Providing effective UA for an iPad is an important part of ensuring customer satisfaction at higher price points. This should be something your team factors into the tablet development budget.

Working with the iPad

When the iPad first came out people joked that it worked like a big iPhone but without the phone. It turns out that the way people use the iPad is a lot different from the iPhone. But under the hood, the technology is very much the same. You can open up an iPad project in Interface Builder using the same tools you use with the iPhone. The simulator also works for the iPad, shown in Fig. 9.8. If you have provisioned an iPad device, it will get added to your list of devices in IB.

Fig. 9.8 An iPhone app displayed in the iPad simulator

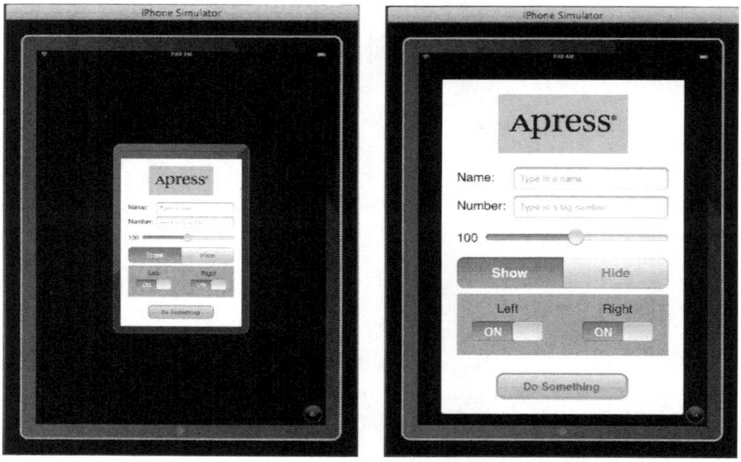

Popover window

One of the few UI elements that is different in iPad is the UIPopoverController. This is a special window that can be anchored to other controls in the UI. The window can be sized as needed and dismissed by the user with a single tap. It is a great place to put Help content. The content can be formatted using HTML/CSS and can include images and links. Fig. 9.9 shows how this was used in the Office HD app — a relatively large popover window.

Your developer can change the size of the popover with the setPopoverContentSize attribute.

Fig. 9.9 A Help topic displayed in a Popover window

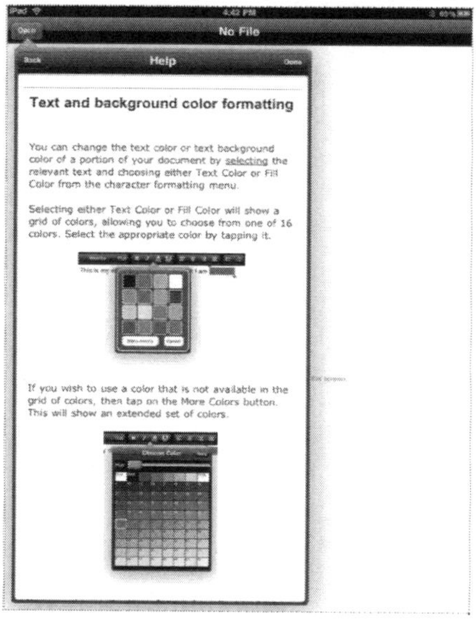

If your application is supported on the iPhone as well as the iPad, you will have some decisions to make regarding how to implement your UA. Many organizations are choosing to produce different UIs for the two devices. This can change your user interface text, the position of Help icons, and Help content.

An example is eTrade which has both iPhone and iPad apps. The iPhone version was discussed earlier in this book on page 25. Each section of the app appears on its own screen. A Help icon is located on the far right end of a lengthy tool bar. The Help page is a list of frequently asked questions and answers.

In the iPad version (Fig. 9.10a) the functional areas of the app are arranged in a more open, flowing style. Navigating between areas is very different from the iPhone version. The Help icon is in a popover menu instead of a menu bar. The icon links to a FAQ (b.) that is similar to the one for the iPhone, but uses different language and topics.

Fig. 9.10 eTrade apps

a. iPad menu b. iPad FAQ

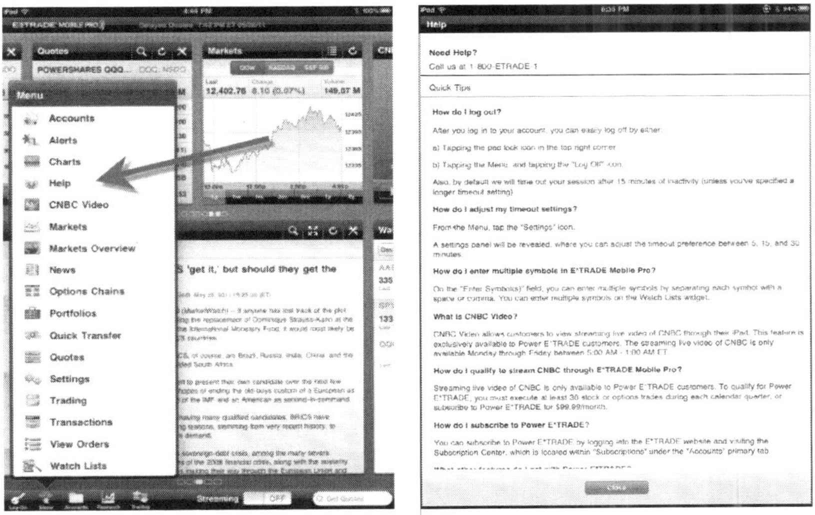

Working with Android-based Tablets

In the Android world, there is an ever-increasing array of devices. Many of these are sized to compete with the iPad in the tablet arena. Android-based tablets are generally between 7" to 10" in height. Google recognized the hybrid nature of tablets; less than a laptop but more than a smartphone. They created a version of Android designed just for tablet use called Honeycomb.

The first release was version 3.0, API level 12. This offered customizable home screens, support for widgets, a larger keyboard, multiple app windows, and Flash support. The most recent release, 3.1, is a major upgrade. Unlike other dot releases for Android, 3.1 did not get a new name. It is still called Honeycomb. The new release has better navigation, support for input devices and other USB accessories, improved standard applications, and the ability to save web pages for offline reading.

Honeycomb works with the same development framework as earlier versions of Android. For Eclipse users, there are new updates to the SDK. This includes a new AVD as shown in Fig. 9.11.

Fig. 9.11 Android Honeycomb

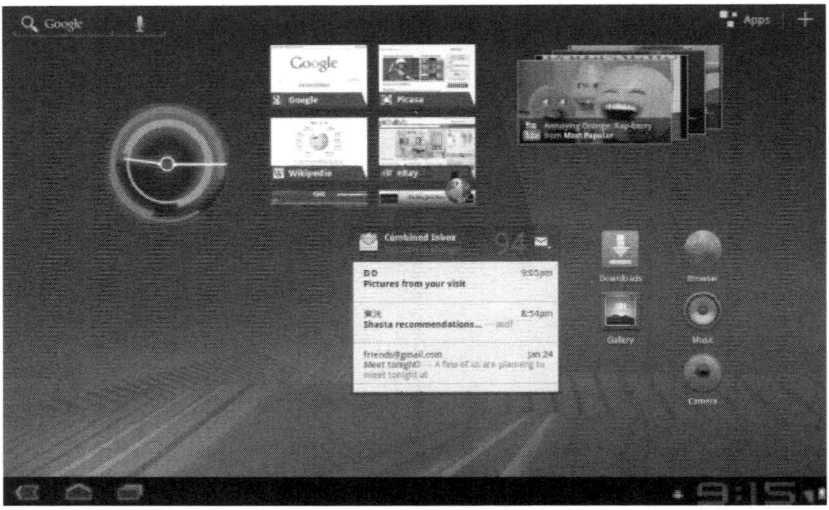

10 Integrating with Other Types of User Assistance

If you are supporting a robust mobile app, you might want or need to consider forms of user assistance outside of the ones discussed thus far in this book. Content types like user interface text, context-sensitive links, guided help (wizards), FAQs, and tips can all be integrated into mobile apps.

Other content types don't work so well. Extensive reference information, blogs, support forums, and knowledge-bases usually fit better in a desktop environment where there is more screen real estate. There are also support options that might be mobile but are not tied directly to an app. This includes social media apps like Twitter, Facebook, and YouTube. It also includes file formats like EPUB and PDF.

The need for external support can manifest itself in other ways. Many corporate mobile apps are created as a supplement to large-scale, more traditional enterprise applications. Usually this implies the need to link, sync, and share data between the two.

In all of these situations, it is important to consider how to help the user move from the mobile app to the external support and back again. It is not a trivial issue. If navigating to Help resources is difficult, users may get frustrated with the app. The best approach is to have a clear plan on what external resources you might want to address before the app design is set in stone.

External mobile support apps

The AutoCAD app shown in Fig. 10.1 is a good example of using external social media apps for product support. AutoCAD has instructional videos on YouTube, a group on Facebook, and a Twitter account. Each of those is delivered by their respective apps. Providing a great user experience requires a lot of effort to design effective offerings in those apps. With apps like Facebook and Twitter, it also means having an official presence with regular updates. The links to these apps are made obvious by grouping the icons on a support page that can be accessed from the AutoCAD app. A "Back" button in the title bar of the social apps makes it easy to get back to the AutoCAD app.

Fig. 10.1 AutoCAD use of external mobile apps for UA delivery

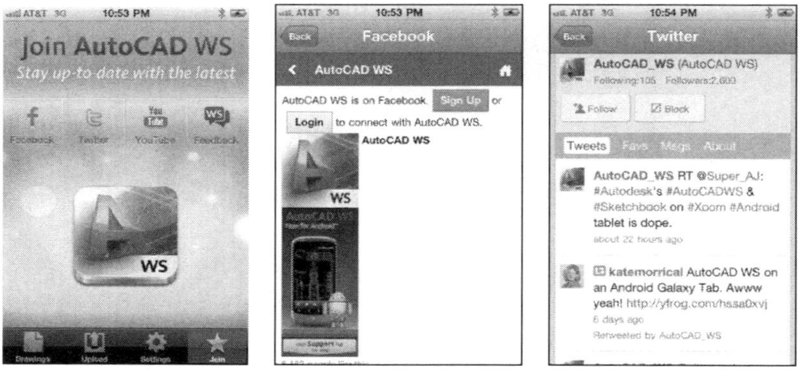

Web-based Help

A web site is a logical place to host detailed information about an app. The trick is to get the user to the site. A common mistake is to link from within an app to a web page that is designed only for viewing through a desktop browser. Refer to the information about this in the Viewport section, page 54.

eBay provides support in the app with Help topics and YouTube videos, as shown in Fig. 10.2a. There is also a link (b.) to the comprehensive Help page on the eBay site. However, that Help page (c.) is not optimized for use in a mobile browser. It does not allow for pinching the page, and this makes it difficult to navigate and read the content.

Fig. 10.2 eBay UA options

a. b. c.

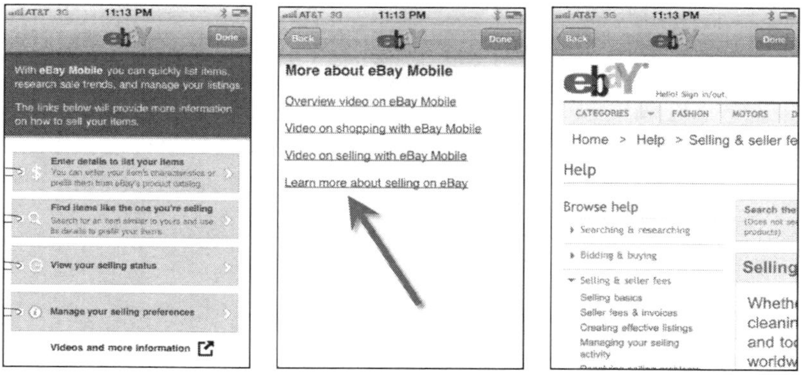

OneNote Mobile, shown in Fig. 10.3, doesn't have any Help embedded in the app. It takes three clicks to get to the OneNote Help page on the Microsoft site. Once there, the topics are arranged in a FAQ with links from the questions to the answers. The content flows well in the mobile window but the text size is very small and uses a faint grey color.

Fig. 10.3 OneNote Mobile external Help page

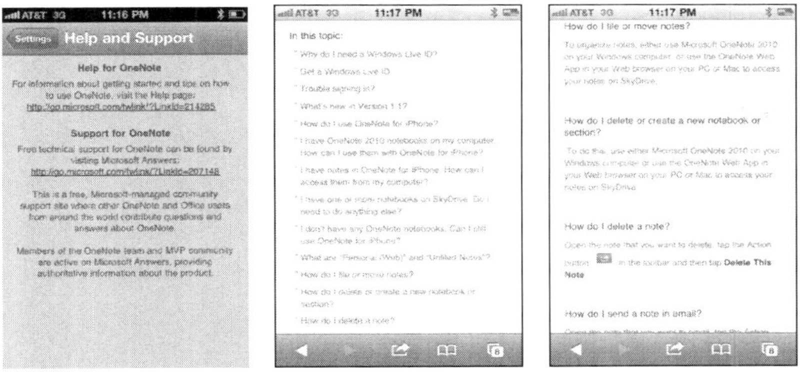

External web site

The Calvetica app has very innovative, visual documentation on its web site, shown in Fig. 10.4. The information takes good advantage of the larger amount of screen real estate. Assuming users have access to a desktop browser, this can be a great way to learn about the products. However, there is no information within the app to let users know that this information is available.

Fig. 10.4 Calvetica desktop Help page

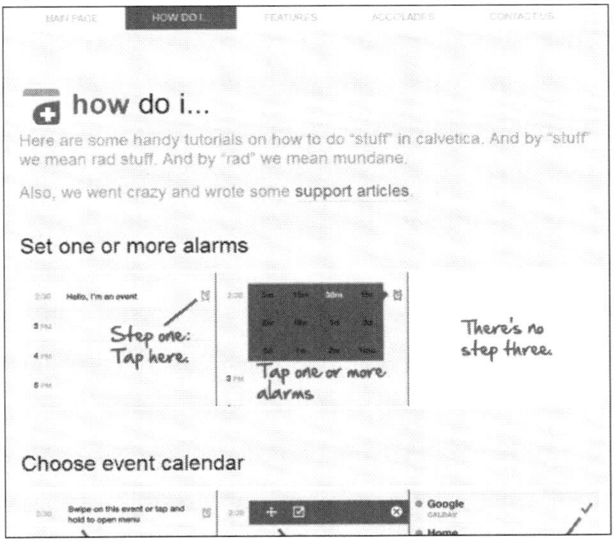

The Evernote app has both a desktop and a mobile version. There is also a web site providing excellent support information for the desktop product. In addition to the documentation, there is a blog and a tips page. For the mobile app they created special versions of the tips and blog, shown in Fig. 10.5a and b. Unfortunately, to find those pages you need to navigate through a very dense page of information with very small type (Fig. 10.5c).

Fig. 10.5 Evernote tips and blog

a. b. c.

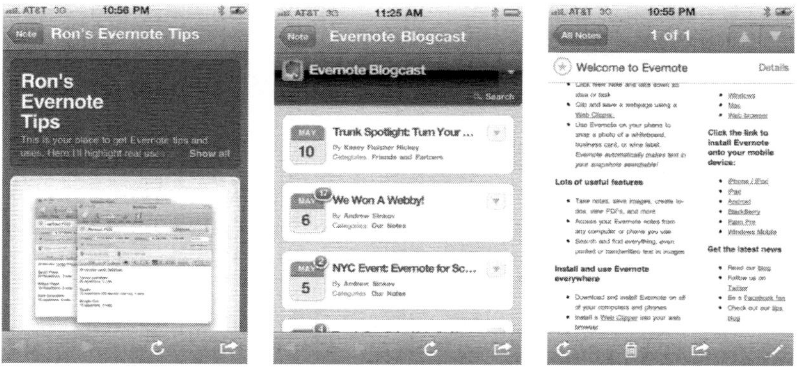

Web-based forums and knowledge bases

Quickbooks has a link from within the app to a community support page. Through the support page, it is easy to ask questions. Answers are often posted from support personnel. Although the support page displays within the app frame, the content has not been optimized for mobile viewing, as shown in Fig. 10.6a. It is impossible to read without a lot of stretching. The same page viewed in a desktop browser is shown in Fig. 10.6b.

Fig. 10.6 Quickbooks Community

a. b.

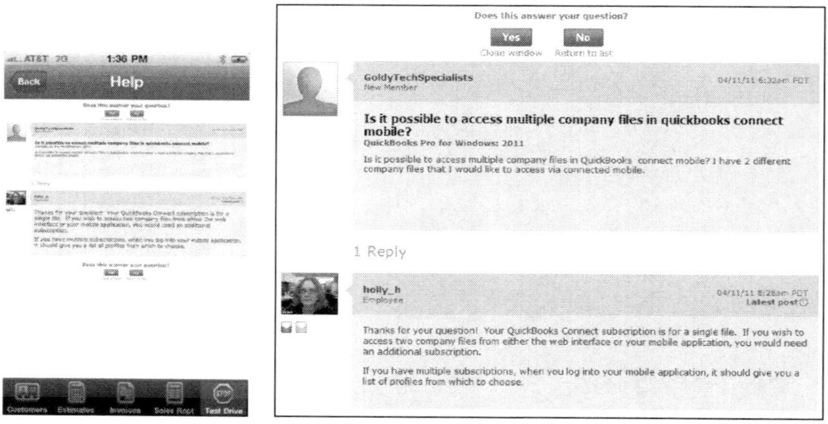

Many software organizations have existing repositories for reference information. It makes sense to build on that when adding in a mobile app. The trick is to do it in a way that makes the content easily accessible to the mobile user. Quickoffice has a great knowledge-base with a lot of good information provided in a variety of formats including PDF and video (Fig. 10.7). One of the problems with the solution is that it is designed for use in a desktop browser. Since the product is designed to be a complement to desktop/laptop computers, this isn't too much of a problem. It would be nice if the topics could be filtered by device and display in the device through some form of link list.

Fig. 10.7 Quickoffice knowledge-base

HP did the right thing by creating a comprehensive support forum specifically for its mobile ePrint app. Shown in Fig. 10.8, it is just one part of a large set of product forums. However, there is no link at all from the ePrint iPhone app to the ePrint topic area in the forum. For that matter there is not even a mention of the forum in the app.

Fig. 10.8 ePrint support forum

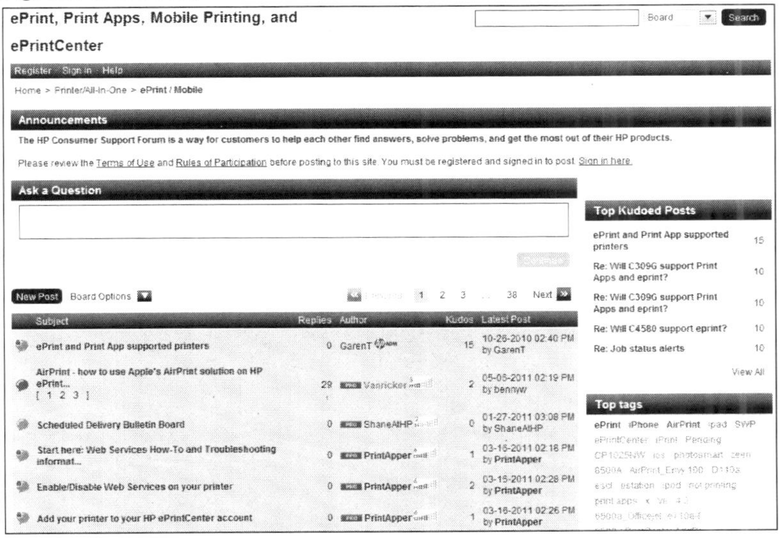

Email support links

Customer contact through email is often provided as a support option for traditional software applications. Its use in mobile apps is no different. The most common implementation is an info page that includes the support email address, as shown in Fig. 10.9. A link can be attached to the email address to automatically display the keyboard and email client when the user clicks on it. ToonPAINT (a.) uses a full page of information describing their email support. Calvetica (b.) includes a link at the beginning of their FAQs. WebMD (c.) uses email to send the user a variety of useful information.

Fig. 10.9 Email support links

a. ToonPaint b. Calvetica c. WebMD

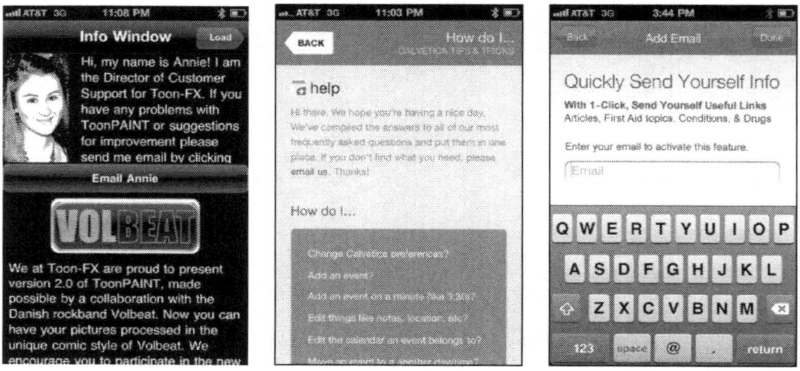

Encapsulated content

There are now a variety of methods for packaging content for digital reading. The Adobe PDF format has been around for a very long time and is well-established. Numerous eReader formats are now available as well. What this technology brings to the table is a content packaging that is optimized for reading sizeable amounts of content on digital devices. It is natural to look to this as an option for delivering UA content in support of mobile devices. All the major mobile operating systems support PDF and eReaders in one form or another. The question is whether they can truly be effective in supporting UA in mobile apps.

PDF: The Portable Document Format is a proprietary technology from Adobe. It is not enabled natively on any mobile platforms. Users need to download a PDF reader and install it on their device. What this means is you can't count on your content being available to your users. Despite this, it is possible to link to a PDF from within an app. It is also possible to link to a specific page in a PDF. However, in practice this is rarely done.

EPUB: This is an open source format for displaying digital books. It has become one of the most prominent formats and is supported by most major eReaders. As with PDF, a mobile device needs to have a supporting eReader installed to view EPUB documents. The readers are readily available. In iOS, Apple aggressively invites users to install iBooks, which supports EPUB. However, you still have no way of knowing whether a particular user will have an eReader installed.

You will need to search far and wide to find examples of mobile apps that are using PDF or EPUB to provide user assistance.

Integrating with a Desktop Application

For mobile apps supporting an enterprise application there is an added element of design and there is much more involved in the implementation. What the user wants is a seamless experience. The type of information on the devices might be different but should feel like part of the same whole. This can be difficult to do. It is likely that the enterprise application has been designed before the mobile app and is well entrenched. It may be tough, but not impossible, to change the user interface to accommodate the mobile app.

There are two areas that are typically involved in connecting mobile and desktop apps: syncing and file sharing. Your developers will determine the process and protocol.

Syncing

When a mobile and a desktop app are designed to work together, it is often possible to synchronize data. A salesperson will want to have the latest contact information; a field service technician needs a list of the day's assignments; a test engineer might be uploading experimental data. The list of possibilities is endless. What all the scenarios share is the challenge of getting one device to link to another.

Generally, this challenge is limited to the first time a user needs to create the sync. There is usually some set up required on each device to authorize the transaction. Often this will include security information. Finally, there is a procedure to initiate the syncing.

You can't underestimate the difficulty this may cause users. Connecting often varies based on operating system and browser type. Troubleshooting information is often needed to deal with those differences as well as wi-fi access, pass codes, and IP addresses.

If setting up the sync is a one-time process, it can be dealt with through a wizard or guided Help. In this case, the user doesn't necessarily need to learn the process. They just need to be able to accomplish it. On the mobile side, it is important to integrate the Help with the app as tightly as possible. It is close to impossible for a user to follow a complicated procedure when switching between an information page and the app itself.

Fig. 10.10 Quickoffice syncing video

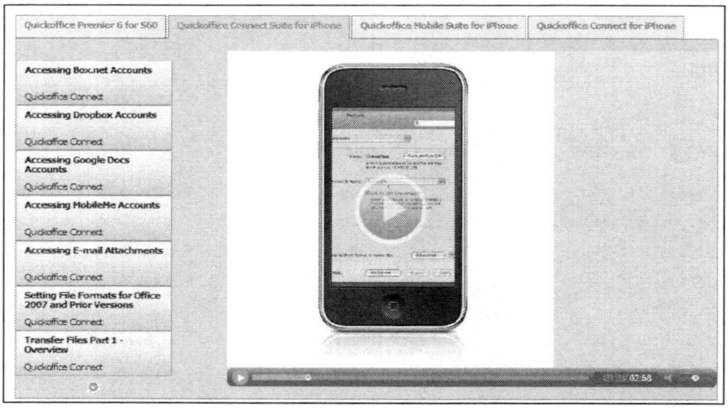

If the user needs to adjust settings on both sides of the sync, then a browser-based procedure or video might be the right solution. The same content page could be viewed from either device. Quickoffice uses a series of videos on their web site for demonstrating syncing (Fig. 10.10).

Manual file sharing

Another integration area you might need to consider is manual file sharing. Many apps use this method instead of automatically synchronized sharing. There will still be a connection between two devices. A screen/page on one or more of the devices will offer some form of a file explorer. A user will typically use that explorer to find a file and initiate the synchronization to the other device.

In iOS, iTunes provides a sharing facility that some developers use. In this case, code in the application tells iTunes that sharing is enabled. The user connects their iOS device to a desktop version of iTunes and navigates to the Apps section. iTunes presents a list of all sharing-enabled apps at the bottom of this page as shown in Fig. 10.11. The user can then moves files between the two devices.

Fig. 10.11 iTunes file sharing

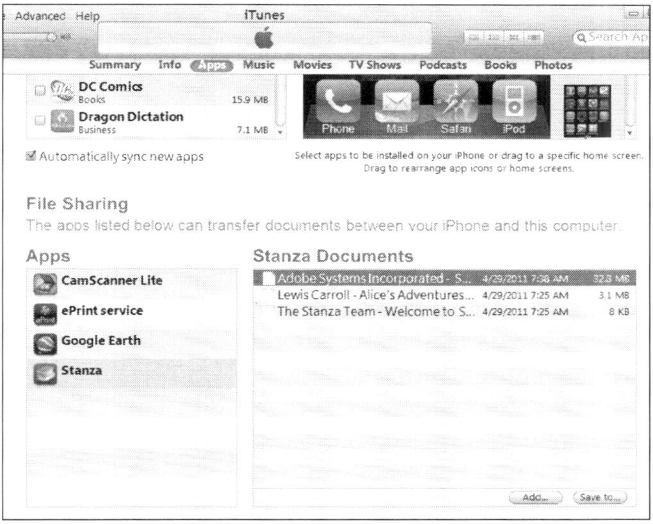

You can find Apple's procedure for this process on the iTunes support site:

- http://www.apple.com/support/itunes/
  Adding and Syncing Content /
  Moving content between your computer and device

Desktop App Stores

The iTunes App Store has had a dramatic impact on the development and sales of software. The success of mobile apps is driving software toward an architecture that functions equally well on mobile and desktop computers. Apple launched its *Mac App Store*, shown in Fig. 10.12. Amazon has the *Appstore for Android*. It appears that Microsoft is working toward something similar for Windows 8. Google will be releasing a marketplace for web-based apps for its Chrome OS laptops.

Desktop hardware is changing as well. Systems like the HP Touchsmart (Fig. 10.13a) employ touch and gestures. The Apple Magic Trackpad (Fig. 10.13b) is bringing touch to desktops as well. The form factor and vocabulary of mobile devices will continue to influence the evolution of larger systems.

Fig. 10.12 Mac App Store

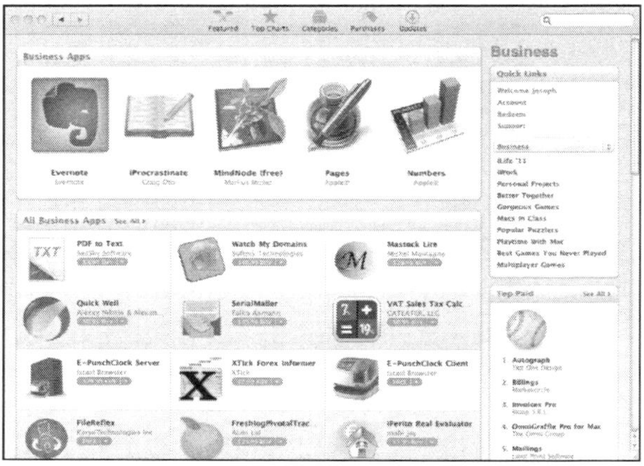

Fig. 10.13 Touch comes to the desktop

a. HP Touchsmart

b. Apple Magic Trackpad

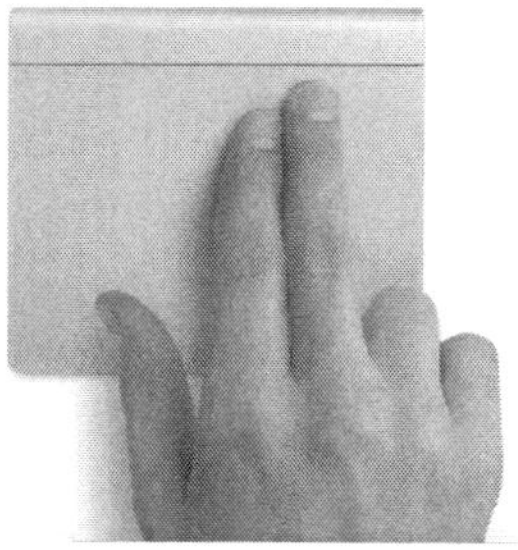

What this is likely to mean for software developers is a blurring of the line between what it means for applications and devices to be mobile or fixed. Mobile apps will be more and more powerful. Desktop apps will get more streamlined and integrate better with mobile. All of this suggests the need for a lot of changes in the design and implementation of software user assistance.

Index

A

AccuTerra, 5
Adobe RoboHelp, 65
Agile development, 10
Amazon, 27
Android
    gallery of button bars, 41
    installation, 86
    SDK, 85
Apollo, 104
App Hub, 102
app stores
    Apple, 1
    desktop, 127
    iTunes, 2
    Mac, 128
AutoCAD, 22, 30, 35, 120
AVDs, 88

B

Backspin Software, 63
Beginning iPhone 4 Development book, 72
Blackberry, 14
browser
    compatibility, 51
    compatibility table, 52
browser-based Help, 51

C

Calvetica, 26, 35, 121, 124
case study
    iPhone User Guide, 43
    Quickoffice, 39
    Timewerks, 38, 41, 53
Chevy Dealer Mobile, 6
Cisco Global Internet, 8
color, 42
conceptual information, 5
content
    conceptual, 5
    creation, 9
    embedding in an app, 69
    hosting on a server, 69
context-sensitive Help, 57
Convertbot, 29, 30, 35
corporate apps, 5, 6, 8
CSS, 9
    example, 54

D

Dashcode, 59
Debug Console, Android, 82
demos, 28
designing UA, 8, 19
Developer Mode in Safari, 66
Developer Registration Tool, 102
Device Chooser, Android, 93
DITA, 10

E

eBay, 22, 25, 35, 120
    videos, 29
Eclipse, 86
eLearning, 10
email support links, 124
emulators, 14
    Android, 91
    iOS. See simulator
    WP7, 99
EpicWin, 22
EPUB, 124
    RoboHelp, 65
ePublisher Platform, 62
eReaders

for EPUB documents, 124
for general reference information, 2
error messages, 46
eTrade, 25, 117
Evernote, 122

F

FAAwait, 28
Fantasia Paint, 45
file sharing, 126
first-time users, 20
Flare, 60
Flash, 9
Ford Sync, 16
forums, 122

G

Galaxy, 107
Gallery
of iPad Help, 84
of iPhone Help, 84
Geotrust, 102
gestures
language of, 33
table of common, 34
Touch Reference Guide, 36
Google
Help, 30
Search app, 23
Grab, 81
guided Help, 22

H

hardware/software requirements
Android, 85
iOS, 71
WP7, 97
Honeycomb, 117
HP ePrint Service, 7, 123
HTML5, 9
test site, 52
Human Interface Guidelines, Apple, 83

I

IBM Mobile Systems Remote, 7
icons, 42
image formats, 49
Infinity Blade, 111
Ingram Micro Mobile, 7
installation
Android, 86
WP7, 97
Intel Retail Edge Program, 8
Interface Builder, 72
internationalization. See translation
iOS
Dev Center, 71
screen captures, 81
SDK, 71
iPad, 15, 115
Popover window, 116
iPhone User Guide, 43
iTunes
app store, 2
file sharing, 126

J

Java, 85
JPG, 49
jQuery, 62

K

knowledge-bases, 122
Kukulska-Hulme, Agnes, 33

L

Language and Communication book, 33
LinkedIn,iPhone Developer group, 83
localization. See translation

M

Mac App Store, 128
MadCap Flare, 60
market share, 14
Media Queries, 56
memory setting for Windows, 87
messaging, 46
Meta tag, Viewport, 54
Meyer, Gordon, 3
MicroStrategy, 113
multi-touch, 4

MyHumana Mobile, 7

N

Nielsen, Jakob, 46, 57
Nodo, 104
Nokia, 14
numbering, of steps, 42

O

Objective-C, 78
Office Word, 45
OneNote Mobile, 121

P

Pastrykit, 64
PDF, 124
periods, use of, 43
Photo Collage, 46
Photocard, 110
PhotoPad, 5, 27, 45, 58
PNG, 49
Popover window, 109, 116
Popplet, 112, 114
procedures, 41
programming languages, 10
    Java, 85
    Objective-C, 78
provisioning
    iOS, 76
Pulse, 111, 114

Q

Quadralay, 62
Quickbooks, 122
Quickoffice, 5, 39, 123, 126

R

Raytheon Jobs, 8
RoboHelp, 65

S

Safari, 78
    Debug Console, 82
    User Agents, 66
Safeco Insurance, 7
screen captures
    Android, 94
    iOS, 81
    WP7, 105
screen size, 4, 109
SDK
    Android, 85
    iOS, 71
    WP7, 97
SDK and AVD Manager, 89
server-based Help, 69
Set My Browser Size web site, 67
setPopoverContentSize attribute, 116
simulators, 14
    iOS, 73
Sketchbook, 113
skills, for mobile development, 8
skins
    Android, 89
    WP7, 100
Skitch, 82
smartphones
    Android, 13
    Blackberry, 14
    iPhone, 13
    market share, 14
    Nokia, 14
    options, 13
    unlocked, 16
    WP7, 14
social media, 10
Sony Xperia Play, 41
SoundHound, 22, 30
Starbucks Mobile Card, 24
steps, 42
Stickyboard, 112
structured authoring, 10
style sheet example, 54
syncing, 125

T

tablets, 15
    Android, 117
    designing UA for, 108
    iPad, 115
    overview, 107
Tasks Anywhere, 46
testing
    apps in WP7, 99

Safari Debug Console, 82
usability, 8
with a provisioned app, 68
with a Windows Phone, 102
with an iOS device, 76
with Safari User Agents, 66
with simulators, 67
testing apps in Android, 91
Timewerks, 26, 38, 41, 53
Today in iOS podcast, 83
tools
authoring, 58
Dashcode, 59
ePublisher Platform, 62
Flare, 60
jQuery, 62
Pastrykit, 64
RoboHelp, 65
testing, 66
Twister, 63
ToonPAINT, 20, 35, 124
TotalConnect, 7
Touchup, 110
Toyota Entune, 16
translation, 10
iOS, 82
issues for gesture terms, 36
tutorials, 47
Twister, 63

U

UI text. See user interface text
Usability Professionals Association, 8
usability testing, 8
case study, 38
user agents
testing with Safari, 66
user interface guidelines (Whatley), 36
user interface text
Android, 93
iOS, 74
WP7, 104

V

versions
Android, 87
Windows Phone, 103
videos, 28, 126
eBay, 29
tutorials, 47
Viewport meta configuring, 55
Viewport meta tag, 54
in WP7, 55
virtual devices, Android, 88
Visual Studio, 98

W

web site, book, 2
web-based Help, 120
WebHelp Mobile, 61
WebKit, 78
WebMD, 21, 124
Weightbot, 21, 35
Windows Phone, 97
versions, 104
WP7
SDK, 97
Writing procedures, 41

X, Y

Xcode, 71
Xoom, 107

Z

Zune, 103

2495808R00086

Printed in Germany
by Amazon Distribution
GmbH, Leipzig